LOVE YOUR LIFE!

The 7 Secrets to Using the Power of Positive Thinking & Law of Attraction to Create the Dream Life for YOU

Written by
Sammy Davis

SammyD.TV

Printed by CreateSpace
ISBN-13: 978-1503238398
ISBN-10: 1503238393

Formatting Editor: Kayleigh Lot
Cover Designer: Pixel Studio on Fiverr
Chapter photos by: Wendy Kissinger Photography
All photos available for purchase on
Society6: society6.com/sammydstyle

Dedicated to

Those who feel alone in this world. You are supported, and we love you for who you are. Thank you for being here. Thank you for your love.

*"I change my life when I change my thinking.
I am Light. I am Spirit.
I am a wonderful, capable being.
And it is time for me to acknowledge
that I create my own reality with my thoughts.
If I want to change my reality,
then it is time for me to change my mind."*
— Louise L. Hay

"What you are seeking is seeking you."
— unknown

Because You Are More Powerful, Beautiful & Special Than You Think

This book is dedicated to you, your life and the fact that you were born a miracle.

I believe that we are all here to create, feel and spread love. It is our inalienable right and when we commit to it, we are actually making the world a better place with our positive energy.

But sometimes "life" gets in the way. We feel bogged down. We feel overwhelmed. We feel uncertain, disillusioned, confused.

I wrote this book because I want to inspire you that you have the power to feel good now, to feel happy now, to feel empowered, inspired and motivated to love your life … NOW!

I also wrote this book because you are OK exactly where you are, and this book will show you why no matter what you've experienced in life, all is perfect, whole and complete and you can create everything out of nothing in this very moment. You only need to choose.

I am so thrilled that you are here. I am so thrilled that you are here not just reading this dedication, but alive, breathing and shining your light on the world.

The world needs, deserves, wishes to see you shine. Thank you for taking a chance to see yourself - the world - and your life another way. A way which, when combined with the power of positive thinking and the law of attraction, is a joy ride of endless possibility, infinite abundance and authentic connection to your highest self.

Welcome. Welcome to the book which just may change your mind - change your life - and change your world.

Contents

Forward

YouAreCreators

When we began practicing the law of attraction the first thing that we had to do was really monitor the way we thought, this not only meant thinking positively but also recognizing when our thoughts did not align with our purpose.

To change your thought pattern you must indeed change everything in your life that is not conducive to your new beginning. In therapy this is called changing people, places and things.

Throughout our journey we have encountered many extraordinary people who have added such beauty to our lives and inspired us to be better people. Sammy is one of these people.

It is said that we are all connected and in life you will encounter people who you immediately feel a strong spiritual connection too. This is the relationship we have with Sammy.

Our relationship initially began as a professional one as we worked together to serve people with a similar purpose. In a short time we have since ventured into a kinship of connected purpose, passion and reason.

This book is truly written by a woman with true wisdom and spiritual vision and is filled with universal love.

We hope this book brings you enlightenment and endless revelation of knowledge.

Infinitely loved,

Justin and Ericka from YouAreCreators
The largest channel for motivation & law of attraction on YouTube

YouAreCreators YouTube Channel: http://www.youtube.com/user/YouAreCreators
YouAreCreators Website:
http://www.youarecreators.org

My Story

"What men and women need is encouragement. Their natural resisting powers should be strengthened, not weakened ... Instead of always harping on a man's faults, tell him of his virtues. Try to pull him out of his rut ... Hold up to him his better self, his real self that can dare and do and win out! ... People radiate what is in their minds and in their hearts."
— Pollyanna

Manifesting a Man — It Can Happen to You

I had just come home from an amazing wedding. My friend Rachel had gotten married in Cape May, New Jersey, a beautiful town with 19th century gingerbread houses that made my heart flutter and a seascape that left me breathless for the blessings of life.

Her relationship with her husband was a marvel to behold. They truly appeared to be better people in one another's presence, and like mirrors, were reflections of happiness, joy and a bright future together.

I was so high from their wedding that upon returning home to my apartment in New York City, I decided to release my extra energy by going on a run in Central Park ... despite it already being 8:30PM in the evening.

So there I was, running miles in the dark of Central Park but feeling like it was as bright as a Caribbean island's day.

During that run, I listened to the Black Eyed Peas and other uplifting music while moving my body to the beat of my legs and the rhythm of my heart. I was literally *high on life* thanks to the positive energy of my friend's wedding. I felt love surging through my legs. It felt like I had given myself a shot of adrenaline!

As I ran that night, I envisioned my soul mate and my life partner appearing before me. I literally *felt* his presence and trusted that, "YES! He was here!" And in that moment, I knew he was here on this planet.

Flashback to a few weeks earlier, when I had spotted an attractive man at a pool in Central Park where I swim.

Every morning at 8AM I noticed him in his Speedo … and yes, he seemed to notice me, too! The silent energy between us was so strong that it would leave me on a high for the rest of the day. My admirer at the pool was literally putting the wind under my sails, with just a few glances as we'd exit the pool after our swims!

Back to my post-wedding run. As I finished my run at Central Park and stared affectionately toward the pool where my mystery man and I were having our morning romance, I thought to myself, *'You know, tomorrow I'm going to introduce myself to him. And we are going to meet one another and go on a date. Because*

I'm worth it and I know that he's interested in me. So you know what? I'm going to introduce myself to him and make this happen!!'

It was in that moment that I decided to meet this mystery man at the pool and that he would want to meet me. There were no ifs, ands or buts. While happily reflecting on this confident decision I had made to introduce myself, I decided to get up from my stretching and walk along the top of the park where it ends at 110th Street.

I felt amazing. And as I reveled in the freedom of this good energy, I looked back at the pool and thought again, *'Tomorrow I will meet him.'*

Literally one second after that thought crossed my mind, I felt a presence beside me. I turned to see what human being had chosen to walk directly up next to me at 9:30PM on a dark summer's night above Central Park.

I looked to my left … and the person I saw?

Why, IT WAS THE MYSTERY MAN FROM THE POOL!

Startled, I immediately said, "Hi … don't you swim at Lasker? (the name of the pool in Central Park)."

He answered that he did, and said hello.

I was shocked into robotic action, immediately sticking out my hand and introducing myself.

It sounds crazy, but it's true.

What happened that evening at the top of Central Park was the manifestation of what I had envisioned myself doing, except I thought it was going to happen the following day.

But the power of attraction had brought him to me in that very moment.

The power of attraction had inspired me to go on that run at 8:30PM. The power of attraction inspired me to sit in the grass and stretch. And when I decided to meet my mystery man, the power of attraction inspired me to get up and begin walking home and within mere seconds meet him … without having to do a single thing.

The mystery man at the pool and I did wind up dating. In fact, on our first date we went surfing at the Rockaway Beach and he kissed me in the waves! Mystery man was also a romantic man - something else I wanted, and believed I deserved, at that time in my life.

I've spent my entire life manifesting and until a few years ago, I thought I was just "keeping the faith" and perseverance on my path. It was, actually, both - the secret sauce of success that's one half what you do, and one half how you feel about doing it and attracting that opportunity into your life.

Perhaps you loved this story and truly believe this story, but you're still doubtful the law of attraction can work for you.

Perhaps you're asking yourself right now: "Why do so many people go through the right motions but don't get the right manifestation they're looking for?"

Here's the simple answer: Because they've only got 50 percent of the ingredients covered. And this book? It'll teach you not just what *to do* - but how *to feel* while you're doing it so that the cake of conscious creation you're baking tastes good, looks good, and serves you the success you've wanted all along.

What You Need for *LOVE YOUR LIFE!*

1. A **pen** you absolutely love using to complete the exercises found inside (I love Sharpie).
2. About **two hours** reading time and up to **10 hours** for completing the exercises.
3. An **open heart and mind.**
4. **Belief** you will learn what you didn't know before.
5. **Commitment** to completing the exercises as an honest, authentic reflection of your inner thoughts and feelings right now.
6. **Acceptance** that the law of attraction is a lifelong commitment and not an overnight transformation.
7. **Love for your life right now** because spirit led you to purchase or receive this gift for your higher good.

Law of Attraction: What It Is

"So Sammy, what is the law of attraction anyway?" is something you may be asking yourself right now.

Before I give basic background on what the law of attraction is and how you can use it, I will first tell you what the law of attraction is *not*.

The law of attraction is not … **a physical, tangible thing.**
The law of attraction is not … **a $97 program for infinite success.**
The law of attraction is not … **getting everything you want overnight.**
The law of attraction is not … **the answer to all of your life's questions.**
The law of attraction is not … **the key to your authentic happiness.**

Those are a few things the law of attraction is *not*. So what are a few things the law of attraction actually *is*?

The law of attraction is … **your energy.**
The law of attraction is … **absolutely free to use or not to use.**
The law of attraction is … **letting go of the "when" and of the "how."**
The law of attraction is … **trusting the universe will aid your highest good.**
The law of attraction is … **celebrating your life and that of others' now.**

A general definition of the law of attraction can be described as the following: *"Like attracts like" and that by focusing on positive or negative thoughts, one can bring about positive or negative results.*

In other words: In order to attract something you want, then you must be at the same vibrational energy of what it is you desire in order to attract that thing toward you.

The law of vibration states that *"Everything that is on the same vibrational frequency makes itself known to each other. When we send out signals on a certain frequency through our thoughts and emotions, the universe responds to us with anything and everything that resonates with that frequency."*

Your positive or negative thoughts therefore act as a magnet attracting people, places, circumstances and knowledge to create a positive or negative experience in the physical realm.

✳ *"You are what you think, not what you think you are."*
— Bruce MacLelland, author "Prosperity Through Thought Force"

Using the power of positive thinking and law of attraction to create the dream life for you is a continuous work in progress because you are always growing and learning more about who you are and what you truly want.

The true power is the power to make a choice at any given moment. So whatever it is you are out to create in the world for the dream life you love, trust that you can become that which you desire because you are all of that already, and more.

Your best life is written in the stars for you. All you must do is decide to live it, and the universe will unfold the necessary elements on your behalf.

Love your life and the law of attraction will lead the way for a *life you love.*

Secret #1

Change Your Self-Concept

"You have brains in your head. You have feet in your shoes. You can steer yourself in any direction you choose. You're on your own, and you know what you know. And you are the guy who'll decide where to go."
— Dr. Seuss

AFFIRMATION

I am already everything I need in order to be who I want to be.

SONG

"I Am" — Christina Aguilera

DEFINITION

Self image (noun): The idea one has of one's abilities, appearance and personality.

IN THIS CHAPTER, WE WILL REVIEW:

1. How I Felt About Me — How I Feel About Me
2. What Is Your Self-Concept?
3. How Do You Feel About Yourself Now
4. Who Would You Like to Believe You Are
5. How to Change the Way You Look At Yourself
6. Why Do You See Yourself the Way You Do?
7. Why It Can Be Hard to Let Go of Limiting Beliefs and Change Your Self-Concept

Who Am I?

You're not supposed to be 100 percent confident.

This is a natural fact of life: What you think and deep down know you can do will still be questioned by a little tiny voice within which says, *'Honey, that seems all well and good, but I just don't think you're ready for that right now.'*

Phooey. You are only ready for what you decide you're ready for - tiny fearful voice or not. Which is why when I realized that I was doubting myself to become the motivational speaker I wanted to be, that I had a choice.

I could either decide to wait and delay my dream.

Or, I could *decide to decide* that I was a motivational speaker and on the path to being paid for speaking engagements, workshops, books and products.

I chose the latter - which is why I'm writing this for you today.

We are each on a path and intuitively we know where we wish to go next on the path, but false limiting beliefs about ourselves will block us from taking those steps.

The key to this chapter is recognizing what you think about yourself and seeing if that lines up with the power, beauty and specialness you truly are for actualizing and attracting what it is you want to do and who you wish to be.

Who Are You?

What do you think about yourself? How do you view yourself and how would you describe your strengths and weaknesses to another person? What conversations are you having with yourself when making decisions, interacting with the world and choosing where to put your attention?

Introspection is the toughest, and most valuable, tool that anyone on the path of self actualization can tackle.

Why? Because the way we view ourselves becomes how we present ourselves to the world and carries the energetic aura to attract, create and manifest our desires. That's why in order to transform our self image, we must first dig deep and know exactly *what* that self image actually is.

If you believe that you are a capable, qualified and intelligent person versus believing you are a stupid, inadequate, struggling soul, your experience as the former is going to be a whole lot different than that of the lesser-than-person.

This is because what you believe is what you achieve. And so if you believe you are capable, you will begin to say, do and attract whatever you need to achieve whatever it is you are certain about.

But if you don't believe you can achieve something, if you don't believe that you've "got what it takes," then what manifests? Exactly that - Nothing. You don't do it, because you don't see yourself as doing it. Without belief there is no behavior.

Here's the good news: Self-image is the most volatile of definitions on the planet.

Why? Because only *you* decide *who* you are. No one else. Not your past, present or so-called future circumstances. None of that matters because your perception is your power if it is you who are creating and attracting everything in your life.

When coaching women through their insecurities and lack-based self concept, what I find over and over again is this little insane belief that they *can't change the way they look at themselves.*

— They believe they can't change the way they view themselves because they've become so *used* to believing whatever stories they've made up about themselves. Because they've chosen to believe it, the story has become true in their physical reality. Because what they see is a reflection of who they feel they are, they can't possibly think that there's anything *but* that definition for them.

How I coach them to see that they are infinite possibility 100 percent of the time is asking them to visualize their best selves, their best lives, their best feelings 100 percent of the time.

I ask them to speak it into existence, write it into existence, and finally - which is the most important - act, believe and behave it into existence.

Here's how you can change your self-image to reflect the biggest, best version of your self you can possibly imagine -

and the steps you need to take to affirm and reaffirm this vision in your mind so that eventually, your reality shifts to physically embody this new story and this new "story" becomes a hit docu-reality TV series called ... *TRUTH!!*

Exercise #1: Who Do You Believe You Are Now

But before we carry on with everything *you truly are* so that you may forget *who you are not,* we do need to show you everything negative you are choosing to believe about yourself.

It's going to be a little icky going to this dark place about yourself. But the good news? Awareness allows you to see, and once you can see, you have the vision to choose again.

It's important I note that you can choose to see yourself however you wish. I'm not going to tell you that your perception is wrong. The purpose of this exercise is to understand how you may be choosing to see yourself in a way which is not serving you and which is not serving your energy level to attract the *the better, the best, the most blessed* for you.

Using the space allotted below each prompt, write the following:

1. **The things I don't like about myself right now are ...**

lack of confidence, insecurities of not being good enough, that mistakes I've made in the past, not letting go, not believing in myself, fear of growing up and taking responsibility, feeling I'm not smart enough, that I have nothing to offer, not knowing who I am, my addiction, how lazy I am, how I procrastinate / lose focus

2. **The fears I have about achieving my greatest dreams are**

Afraid of failing, that it went be enough, that I will went move, afraid of my limitation holding me back to succeed.

3. **The reality I am in which I do not like is …**

that I am a recovy cocaine addict and I have to constantly remind myself of it cause I've gotten so good at hiding it from my self, that I hate myself and don't know how to love myself cause I never have and I worry that I never will

4. **The reasons this reality are true for me is because …**

maybe I am in denial still cause its easier to deny it then to face it and there be some chance of self love. I guess I want to be normal but I never will be and nothing is wrong with that

5. **I am a victim in my life because of these circumstances/ people …**

My childhood/past
Myself

* * *

Exercise #2: Who Would You Like to Believe You Are

Write an obituary of your life after having lived 90 full, fabulous years.

Describe what you did. Your accolades. Your fantastic endeavors, travels, experiences. Your beautiful family, relationship and professional partnerships.

Describe how you were in your life. Were you happy? Were you exciting? Were you serious? Were you recognized? Were you driven? Were you peaceful? Were you a family woman or man? Were you a free bird? Were you a founder, a creator, an artist?

Describe the person you wish to see staring back at you in the mirror on the day you pass into another life.

This exercise will help you to look back on your life and share what it is you wish to be remembered for - and in this moment, what you would like to affirm and believe you can do forever moving forward.

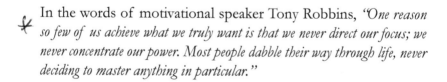 In the words of motivational speaker Tony Robbins, *"One reason so few of us achieve what we truly want is that we never direct our focus; we never concentrate our power. Most people dabble their way through life, never deciding to master anything in particular."*

Here are some questions you can address:

- What is it that you achieved in your life which you are most proud of?
- Did you leave children behind? Did you have a wife/ husband?
- Did you volunteer?
- Did you travel?
- Did you launch your own business or work in the arts?

- Did you win awards and receive accolades?
- Were you loved? Honored? Respected? Revered?

Some people have told me that this exercise makes them feel sad, as if they don't have *enough* time to get everything done in their lives.

But again, in the words of Tony Robbins, *"Once you have mastered time, you will understand how true it is that most people overestimate what they can accomplish in a year - and underestimate what they can achieve in a decade!"*

How will you know which obituary is the one for you?

You'll feel excited. You'll feel energized. And perhaps, you'll feel a little fearful.

Because when you begin to see what it is that you want to be remembered as on the day you die, you remember how precious life is, you remember how priceless life is, you remember why it's so worth seizing the day and living the day as if it were your last.

I hope this exercise reveals who you truly want to be and who you truly are, while inspiring you to take steps toward those goals with action *today*.

Remember, this is your obituary. This is your story. How do you want it to read? How do you want to be remembered? What is your legacy on this planet and what would make you smile with content as you look on the planet from heavenly clouds above?

Use the space allotted below to write.

_____

_____

_____

_____

_____
_____
_____
_____
_____
_____
_____
_____
_____
_____
_____
_____
_____

* * *

_____

Exercise #3: Speaking to Yourself as if You Were This Person

Find a mirror.

Yes. *You.* Go find a mirror, stand in front of it or hold it in front of your face, and begin to speak to yourself like the person you truly, awesomely are.

Speak to your *power.*
Speak to your *talents.*
Speak to your *beauty.*
Speak to your *intelligence.*
Speak to your positive *choices.*
Speak to your right *choices.*
Speak to your *opportunity.*

Speak to your *abundance*.
Speak to your *wealth*.
Speak to your loving *family, friends and support group*.
Speak to your *beautiful home*.
Speak to your *fun, pleasure and relaxation time*.
Speak everything you've ever wanted to yourself - as *decided and declared by yourself*.

Here's how to complete this exercise step-by-step:

1. Stand in front of a mirror or hold a hand mirror in front of yourself.
2. Look at yourself in the eyes.
3. Smile!
4. Take a deep breath.
5. **BEAUTY:** Tell yourself how beautiful you are. Your eyes. your nose. Your cheeks. Your hair. Your skin. Your lips. Your nails.
6. **POWER:** Tell yourself how powerful you are. How you can create everything you've ever wanted, and more. How you can create a great dinner to a great smile to a great relationship to a great (insert creative project here). Tell yourself that you are infinite potential to create infinite opportunity in your life. *Yes! That is you!*
7. **SPECIAL:** Tell yourself how special you are. How you were born a miracle. How you were a unique being destined to be a piece of human flesh on this planet. You were born to shine. You were born to radiate whatever it is you love to do, be and express to the world. Tell your reflection that the world *needs* you!
8. **YOUR DREAMS:** Tell yourself everything about your dreams. Speak in the affirmative: *'I want this to happen. I believe this will happen for you. I know this will*

happen for you. I trust this will happen for you. I see this happening for you!' Give your reflection motivation, as if you were your own coach.

9. **YOUR IMMEDIATE DESIRES:** Tell yourself that what you want right now is here right now. Tell yourself that the extra couple hundred dollars you'd like to have is here. Tell yourself that the good feelings you'd like to have all the time are here now. Tell yourself that the new car, the vacation, the amazing home with a short commute to work is here, *now!* Whatever immediate top of mind desires you have, tell yourself you've got it.

10. **YOUR TALENTS:** Tell yourself everything you're good at doing. Tell yourself everything you've ever done that required talent. Tell yourself a list of the great things you've done. Tell yourself about that awesome time when you accomplished something amazing, or how you are always so good at doing this, or perhaps the fact that everyone needs you for this special skill only *you* have. Remind yourself why you rock.

11. **YOUR SUCCESS:** Tell yourself how successful you are. Tell yourself how abundant you are. Tell yourself that you are in the newspaper. Tell yourself that you are on TV. Tell yourself that you just won an award for your gifts, personal success or work. Tell yourself that you are receiving emails and Facebook messages from old friends congratulating you for all the amazing things you're doing and that they are just *so* impressed and by the way, can you tell them how to achieve like you, too?

12. **YOUR OPPORTUNITY:** Tell yourself that you are unlimited opportunity. Tell yourself that you are *so much* opportunity that you can *turn down* opportunity. Tell yourself that if you were a cup of opportunity,

you'd be overflowing! You have so much opportunity that you have to literally pour out that cup. *Pour out that cup, baby! It's overflowing!*

13. **YOUR PEACE:** Tell yourself how peaceful you are on your path. How every moment is pure bliss. How every moment is pure magic. How everytime you breathe, you breathe in peace, power and patience. Tell yourself that you trust everything you want is on its way. Tell yourself that because you want it, because you believe it, it is coming. Tell yourself that you can effortlessly receive and that your peace is your power.

14. Keep going. Whatever comes up for you, communicate it to yourself.

15. By now you may have become emotional. Grab a box of tissues.

16. Cry. It will make you feel better!

17. Smile. *See!* I told you that you'd feel better.

18. You are all of these things, and more. I believe this for you - and you now you believe it for you, too.

Why Do You See Yourself the Way You Do?

This is a tough question for most people to answer. They don't want to admit that they have been choosing to see themselves as unworthy or victims to their circumstances. They don't want to admit that actually, they *are* good enough to be and attract the things they wish in their life. That it only takes one person to change their lives: themselves.

Because when we begin to take ownership for how we feel, what we do and what we attract, we declare that *we are responsible*. We declare that actually, if it's meant to be, it's up to me.

The reality of who you are is never "determined" by the world around you ... *it is determined by you.*

The reality of what you do is never "regulated" by the world around you ... *it is decided by you.*

The reality of how you feel is never "controlled" by the world around you ... *it is consciously chosen by you.*

Yes, old habits of who you are and the way you behave take time to break and mold and evolve.

Yes, sometimes there's limited time and resources to "do" what you want ... but there's always enough time and resources to take at least one tiny step forward.

Yes, sometimes we are hurt, sometimes we are bruised, sometimes mean things are spoken or done to us.

But all of what is done to us is a gift we choose to receive or dismiss. And someone else's pain is always a reflection of their own. Rather than feel hurt by what they've said, we can feel sorry for them, walk away and wish them the best.

This book will show you how to change your self-image, as well as show you how to *keep changing* your self-image … because the old thought patterns and victim mentality will rear its ugly head as your life progresses.

But guess what? You're in the best place possible. Because after exercises number 1-3, you've not only identified the limiting beliefs you have about yourself, but you talked yourself into an entirely new state of being.

Rather than feel weighed down by your limiting beliefs, you feel empowered knowing that they are *not you*. They are just an idea you have about yourself and you can re-write that idea in any moment you choose.

When you rewrite the ideas you have about yourself, you begin to see who you could declare yourself to be and feel the radical change which comes with making that declaration.

And from this place of faith and confidence in who you are, you will create, you will attract and you will be all of that *and more*.

Why It's Hard for People to Let Go of Their Negative Self Image

<u>Your Past Circumstances</u>

So often we look to what happened in the past to define what we believe can happen in the future.

Let me break it down for you: The past has no meaning. The past, because it is in the past, does not exist. Nope. Never happened. There's *nothing* in the past which you need to create or concentrate on today.

I know. It sounds radical, and you're probably thinking right now, *'Sammy … seriously. The past IS everything! The past is how I am where I am now! Without the past, I wouldn't be where I am today!'*

Well … duh. You just answered my own point: The past led you to where you are now, because you decided to use it as ground for every step you chose to take.

Don't get me wrong: You may have a *great* life! You have money in the bank, a good job, a loving relationship, a stimulating environment.

And these present circumstances, at least before you read this book, were determined by your consciousness of the past which for you, was most likely a reflection of what you're living today.

For example: I was raised in a middle-to-upper class, white, suburban and college-educated family. My father owned a family business and my mom worked her way up the corporate ladder of a local bank.

My family instilled values of hard work, getting an education and making save, practical choices for my life ahead. They also, bless them, showed me a path of independent thought and the freedom to choose.

Which is why my college and early 20s were a reflection of this upbringing. I completed my responsibilities. I worked hard. Graduated with honors. Got a job immediately after graduating. Independently paved my way to living and working in New York City. And if I hadn't decided to carve out a different future for myself, I would have stayed on the path of working the 9 to 5, dating until I "met the one" and immediately stepping into the conversation of stable home, happy family and a 401K retirement fund.

I decided at a young age that wasn't for me in my 20s or early 30s. It was the reality for my parents, but it wouldn't be the reality for me, despite what impressions my past upbringing may have had on me.

So what I am here to teach you is a new way of living your life - a way which needs *no* past to determine *all* present and *all* future.

I don't know your upbringing, but I do know something about

your past has determined your present circumstance.

One simple example of how the past could have determined your present circumstances is your education. Say you have a nursing degree, and did well on your tests.

Logically, you would look to this "past" as reason to decide you should be a nurse, believe that you have the qualifications to be a good nurse and that you'll find a supportive working environment with steady income, time off and benefits.

You believe all of this is possible and because of that belief based on your past, chances are you will become *exactly that* because based on your educational experiences and decisions, this is what led to your self-image which created your present and future success in the industry.

But what if you said something completely different: That you could become a famous rock and roll star. And what if *nothing* in the past would point to this reality. You have *no* training. You have *no* connection to the rock and roll industry. You have *no* understanding of even how to play a chord on a guitar.

But despite all of these limiting circumstances, let me remind you again: The past does *not* matter. So you start with your belief that you are a famous rock and roll star. And you think to yourself, *'Well, what does a rock and roll star need to become a rock and roll star?'*

And you start there. You do not start with the negative thought,

'I've never had a musical training in my life.'

Rather, you start with the *yes*, not the *no*. And the yes is that you can figure out what steps you need to take *now* in order to become that rock and roll star.

Will it be easy as *1, 2, 3, A, B, C?* No.

Was getting your nursing degree easy? No.

So, the choice is yours. But behavior to learn what you need to do and do what needs to be done? That comes from belief. So the first choice to doing anything, then, is believing you can do it.

You tell yourself - *now!* - that you are a famous rock and roll star because that's what you want to be now. Because the only moment which matters, truly, is now.

Exercise #4: What Can You Do Now?

When coaching women to create new self-concepts of themselves without referencing the past, I ask them to focus on the present in these ways.

Use the space allotted below to answer these questions to focus on what you can do *now* to begin attracting what it is you wish to create in your life.

1. What can I do *now?*

_____

_____

_____

_____

_____

_____

2. What can I do to plan my plan *now?*

_____

_____

_____

_____

_____

_____

3. How can I describe this role, accomplishment, position, attraction, etc. *now?*

_____

_____

_____

_____

_____

4. Why is this role, accomplishment, position, attraction, etc. possible *now?*

_____

_____

_____

_____

_____

5. **What is the best thing I can do to take a step toward creating this role, accomplishment, position, attraction, etc.** *now?*

_____
_____
_____
_____
_____
_____
_____
_____

Your Current Circumstances

People believe that they are defined by their circumstances and that making a change from these circumstances is hard, laborious, or next to impossible.

Your current circumstances may be positive circumstances or negative circumstances. It all depends, of course, on your perception of your current reality.

If you happen to be in positive circumstances, desiring or making choices for change may seem silly at first. You may be thinking to yourself, *'If you've got it so good, why would you want it any other way?'*

And then there are the negative circumstances. Those are the ones that people find excruciatingly difficult to overcome and re-define.

Say you are a minority in a situation. You may feel that due to your circumstances, you are without the same opportunities as those who are in the majority.

Or let's pretend you don't have a lot of money to invest in your education, business or home. This may lead you to believe that because you aren't "well off" to begin with, that it will be incredibly difficult to gain the financial freedom you dream about.

Because your current circumstances lack the capital to create a return on investment, you see no other options to create wealth because you believe it takes wealth to create wealth.

And then there's the *'I'm ugly, I can't change the way I look, and I will never be considered pretty.'* Perhaps you don't look like Heidi Klum or Beyoncé on the cover of a magazine. Neither do I. But I believe I'm pretty - because I *say* so. I believe I'm beautiful - because I *feel* so.

The reason our current circumstances can feel difficult to redefine is that they are usually a part of us which we've decided is permanent and unchangeable.

But the most permanent circumstances *can* be changed and evolve for the better with a change in perception, be it of ourselves, our past circumstances or our reality as a whole.

* * *

TAKEAWAY TIP: Use this quote to remind
yourself how your perception creates your
physical reality: *"When you change the way you look*
at things, the things you look at change."
— Wayne Dyer.

* * *

Your Energetic Surroundings

The people you choose to surround yourself with should match the energy you wish to attract and create in your life.

A famous statement is that you are "only as high as your flock." So if you're flying low to the ground in all arenas of your life, take a moment to examine the energy flow of your social circle.

Are the members of your circle flying low to the ground as well? Are they radiating negative energy? Complaining? Are they seeing the glass as half empty? Do they struggle to pay the bills, get the raise they want, or happily transition to a new job? Do they have healthy relationships with themselves, their lovers and their families?

It's important to consciously create a life we love by proactively creating who we are influenced by and what energy most frequently surrounds us. This is because whatever and whoever is near us will radiate energy which we subconsciously absorb - whether we want to or not.

If we wish to give out positive energy, it's in our best interest to align ourselves with people who do that, too. Because if we want to radiate good vibes and live in good vibes ourselves, it will become so much easier when the person before us is a mirror of that which we are already desiring.

The power of attraction is elevated when we are surrounded by those who vibrate on the same energy level of positivity and opportunity.

* * *

TAKEAWAY TIP: Limit your time with people who are what I like to call "energy suckers." You know they're energy suckers because after spending time with them, you feel worse than before or begin to vibrate on feelings of lack, doubt or fear. If you must spend time with them, arrange it so that there's a group setting. The energy of a group will dissipate the negative vibes of one individual so it's not as impactful.

* * *

Your Positive vs. Negative Media Consumption

Do you find yourself cringing every time you turn on Facebook because the news feed is so cluttered with negative energy, news and self-loathing or judgements?

Social media can be a cease pool of icky juju. Thanks to the algorithm of Facebook, my feed reflects the shares from people who have similar positive energy as me. But every now and again there will be someone who posts a personal complaint or fear that triggers me.

The same can be said of the news, film and articles we read. Ever notice that the news is *rarely* happy? This is because people's natural inclination is to uncover pain and suffering. The human curiosity wants to know what wrong is going on in the world.

Which is why positive thinking, energy and living is a conscious decision, or else we'd be seeking out the hardships instead of the happiness by accidental default.

Why do we seek out the bad? It stems back to our most primal days. When we were hunter-gatherers, emergencies had to be tended to immediately for survival. According to the article "Why We Love Bad News" from *Psychology Today*, our primal brains were programmed to focus fully on the fear so that we would stay alive. Unfortunately today, the neurons in our brains react similarly despite the news rarely affecting our direct well-being.

Absorbing negative news therefore triggers our stress hormone, which can put us in a temporary state of depression. And feeling depressed leads to decisions not made from a positive place of self-confidence, care and loving thoughtfulness. When we are stressed, we are agitated, rash and most importantly, make decisions from a place of fear which may not align with our intentions for a powerful, beautiful and special life.

The news, because it skews toward publicity of the bad, keeps us in a place of *feeling bad*. Our minds are trained to "look for the worst." So rather than look to the world as a loving, trusting place, we look to the world as a place which can, will and wants to hurt us.

And the law of attraction, because it is attracting what you believe is true for you, will attract those circumstances, continually reaffirming what it is that you fear most.

We can't hide from the news forever, but we can see it and recognize in our minds that we have a choice: To allow it to scare it us, or to let it motivate us to be more powerful and positive today, because life truly is *now*.

* * *

TAKEAWAY TIP: Experiment with a 30-day news and social media fast. Much like you would with a juice fast, the before and after effects will show you how best to limit your news absorption so that you stay in a place of positive emotional well-being.

* * *

The Thoughts You Choose Not to Think

The scenario: You're looking to create a new job opportunity with increased salary, increased creative responsibility and a shorter commute to work.

Listed are examples of thoughts which you may or may not choose to think in order to create this job with a specific set of requirements.

Exercise #5: Your New Dream Job — What You Can Choose to or Not to Think

1. It's going to be really hard to find a job. I'm going to have to put a lot of work into this.
2. Finding a job that pays this much money isn't possible. I'm going to aim for this (lesser than you deserve) amount of money.
3. My parents said it'd be difficult for me to apply to these high level jobs, so I won't bother putting in the work since it's probably a waste of my time.
4. People like me who have been out of work for weeks aren't usually viewed as qualified candidates.
5. I have everything I need to make the job of my dreams a reality and I'm committed to making it happen.
6. I can create an action plan of steps to apply and attract the job opportunity of my dreams. I have the energy and passion to make this happen because I deserve it for me.

Which of these thoughts seem disheartening?
Thoughts #1 and #2.

Which of these thoughts seem realistic and worth thinking?
Thoughts #3 and #4.

Which of these thoughts seem opportunistic and uplifting?
Thoughts #5 and #6.

Most of these thoughts seem perfectly logical - if not realistic - to think.

But the truth is that with the exception of thoughts #5 and #6, they do not support a flow of positive energy to create a life you truly love.

Many of these thoughts are based on thinking small, using past circumstances to determine current beliefs and in the grand scheme of things, *settling*. In a lot of ways, they are also fear-based.

You can begin to see how in some ways, these thoughts keep you vibrating in fear, which paralyzes and therefore prevents you from actualizing your greatest desires.

While many people in your life may even speak some of these thoughts to you, remember that what everyone else gives you permission to believe ... *you don't have to believe!!*

Be a rebel. Rebel against the madness of fear. Because you are more powerful, beautiful and special than you think, so you don't need to even go where some of these thoughts take you - which is nowhere.

* * *

⚹ **TAKEAWAY TIP:** You can think whatever you want about whatever you want - but it's what you choose *not* to think which, in the end, creates space for the positive beliefs, positive reinforcement and enthusiastic empowerment you can choose to create for yourself.

* * *

Secret #2

Shift Your Energy

"Love one another and help others to rise to the higher levels, simply by pouring out love. Love is infectious and the greatest healing energy."
— Sai Baba

AFFIRMATION

I am a being of positive energy. I am a believer in positive energy. I am a receiver, giver and manifestor of positive energy.

SONG

"I Gotta Feeling" — Black Eyed Peas

DEFINITION

Energy (noun): The strength and vitality required for sustained physical or mental activity.

IN THIS CHAPTER, WE WILL REVIEW:

1. My Energy is My Enthusiasm
2. What Is Your Energy Field?
3. How to "See" Your Energetic Thoughts
4. Why Does Your Energy Matter?
5. Why Energy is a Feeling
6. The Different Levels of Energy
7. Love is All That Matters
8. Love vs Fear, and How to Let Go of Fear

The Energizer Bunny is You

When you are in a state of feeling good, you attract more good things to you. This means you see the good in people. You feel the good in people. You hear and receive the good in people.

You can be in a place of high energy and simply walking into a grocery store when all of a sudden, someone offers you a free sample!

You can be in a place of high energy and you're at the gym and suddenly, you see someone you were just thinking about yesterday ... as if they magically appeared!

You can be in a place of high energy, feeling good and blessed and abundant and then *voila!* You turn your head in just the right direction to spot a $20 bill on the ground for your picking.

Your energy is your aura. Your aura is defined as "An emanation surrounding your body, viewed as the essence of individual."

Your essence can be either negative or positive, and so your aura resides in either this negative or positive state at all times. When you feel yourself in a positive aura, anything good is possible. People are attracted to you. They are lifted higher by your energy.

Ever notice how a sad person will bring you down to their level? As mentioned in Secret #1, the people you surround yourself with have energy which will rub off on you.

The same can be said for your energy level: It will either positively or negatively attract people, circumstances, choices and connections toward you.

Your energy is your power. It will either bring people *up*, or bring people *down*. It will either attract more good things toward you, or attract consciousness or creation of something which is not so good.

Who do you want to be surrounded by? Change your energy to attract more of what you want to be in your positive field of creation, because you create the world around you with the energy you are radiating at any given moment.

What Is Your Energy Field?

Knowing what your energy field consistently is will help you to understand how you are attracting or repelling things in your life.

So often, people who feel bad don't know they are in this default state of being negative. As mentioned in Secret #1, they choose to be a victim. They choose to be a victim because it's where they have the least amount of power to change. So, to be in a negative state is truly to give up on yourself and to relinquish all power that you naturally have.

So how do you know what energy field you're currently in?

By being a witness to your thoughts.

Your thoughts determine how you see the world. Your thoughts determine how you choose to see the world and therefore how you naturally react to the world, which determines what you receive, create and attract.

So being able to witness your subconscious thoughts will help you to see what energy field you are calibrating in.

To "calibrate" in an energy field means that you are literally *buzzing* on this energy. You are feeling the moment(s) and seeing the moments through the lens of this energy.

So if you are feeling bad about a recent breakup, you will be calibrating in the energy of *that sadness.*

You'll see a couple walking hand in hand down the street and feel bad about your current situation. Perhaps you may even feel angry at them, or jealous. This emotion is your reaction and you justify it, *'I just went through a nasty breakup!'* you may think to yourself, *'That's not fair they are in love and I'm not!'*

Because you're calibrating in a negative state, you'll feel anything but happy for them, which is how you'd feel if you were in a happy, joy-filled relationship yourself. In fact, if it weren't for the breakup, you probably wouldn't have even noticed the couple to begin with!

More often than not we don't realize when we're subconsciously calibrating in a negative *or* positive place. The reason for this is because we don't realize how much our thoughts create our reality.

✔ Since we don't "think" about "what we're thinking," we believe they need no questioning. Because we accept everything *we think as just what it is*, we lack the awareness that we can step back and be an observing witness to them and if so inclined, choose to change them.

To be a witness is to separate yourself so that your thoughts do not define you. They can still come up for you (like when you see a happy couple and become sad), but when you learn to recognize they are there, you automatically disconnect yourself from their energy level. By becoming a witness you create space and therefore clear the energetic air, allowing you to choose how you wish to feel and what you wish to think in this moment versus the subsconscious default.

In order to know what it is we are really thinking we must literally "step back" to have an omnipresent view of how our thoughts are speaking to us and dissect the emotion and energy in which they are rooted.

Before proceeding further, I want to walk you through an exercise which allows you to see your thoughts and be an observing witness of them at this very moment.

As you experience this exercise, your thoughts may have nothing to do with this book. Your thoughts may be about other situations, circumstances or expectations circling in your mind about your life.

Your naturally occurring thoughts reflect what you are attached to and because you are attached, you can't break free, and so they easily arrive at your doorstep without you even needing to send them a ride to show up.

Exercise #1

<u>How to See Your Thoughts</u>

1. Find a comfortable place to sit cross legged. Ideally, you are sitting on the floor in a private, nearly-silent space.
2. Cross your legs and straighten your back. Gently fold your hands together in your lap, one hand over the other.
3. Close your eyes and take three deep breaths. Hold each breath for five seconds, and then release. Feel the peace and serenity naturally emerge from your heart-center.
4. Feel the weight of your body on the floor. Feel the way the air floats across your skin. Hear the ambient noise and the sound of your breath entering and exhaling from your nose.
5. Set a timer for five minutes.
6. Sit in stillness for at least five minutes and do your best to focus on your body and your breath without consciously thinking. You are *not* sitting to meditate and remove thoughts. You are sitting to be still and silent in your physical body so that you can hear what is not still and silent in your "monkey" mind.
7. After five minutes is up, grab a pen and some paper and write down what thoughts naturally emerged for you.
8. What did you think about? Who did you think about? Were your thoughts rooted in fear or excitement? Anticipation or angst? Were you thinking of negative things or positive things? Were you criticizing someone else or yourself? Were you celebrating yourself or someone else?
9. Use the space allotted below to write your replies to #7. Take at least five minutes for this exercise.

_____

_____

_____

_____

_____

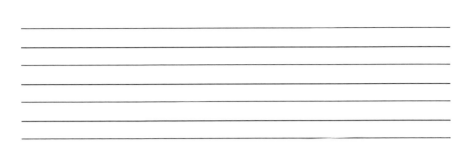

10. Re-read what you wrote down. Were most of these thoughts positive, or were most of these thoughts negative? It's said that to have a healthy relationship with your life partner, that you have five positive experiences to one negative. Is this similar to your ratio, or were you closer to five negative thoughts to one positive one?

11. This exercise shows your relationship to yourself, and how you skew either *more negative* or skew *more positive* in your resting thought patterns.

* * *

The thoughts which entered your mind naturally are indicative of the energy which is buried deep within you. It is the energy which you may not know is there, but thanks to this exercise, was revealed to you.

Chances are you had some negative energy thoughts and some positive energy thoughts. To have a majority of positive thoughts is ideal for a consistent vibration of attracting more of that positive energy. To have a majority of negative thoughts is ideal for a consistent vibration of attraction for more of that negative energy.

So depending on what you wrote down, were you drawn to more negative thoughts, or were you drawn to more positive thoughts?

In the most simplistic of terms remember how the law of attraction is defined in the first place: "Like attracts like."

* * *

TAKEAWAY TIP: As you go about your day, choose to see your thoughts. When a thought emerges which triggers you to "feel" something, take a step back and look at this thought. Where is it coming from? Is it serving your higher good and state of feeling good? Is it even true to begin with? The more you practice being a witness, the less your thoughts stay with you and the more you are able to separate yourself from them and become a compassionate witness.

* * *

Why Energy Matters and Creates Everything

Energy is everything.

The ideal state of energy is a flow of positive. Even when times are tough or we hit turbulent bumps as life will inevitably present us, we still have this tiny wise voice which allows us to know that a better day is on its way. That we get to choose how our future will feel and how even, in the midst of pain and struggle and hardship and loss, we can choose to believe we are being positively guided.

But that's for another chapter. Right now, we simply need to affirm what energy is and why it matters for the creation of anything and everything.

Albert Einstein is credited with saying, "Everything is energy and that's all there is to it. Match the frequency of the reality you want and you cannot help but get into that reality. It can be no other way. This is not philosophy, this is physics."

Coming from one of the smartest men in the history of the planet, it's hard not to trust this statement or at the very least, become curious as to how your life could potentially change for the better if you began to use principles behind the law of attraction.

Energy is defined as strength or vitality for a desired activity, but in the physics world, it is defined as "the property of matter and radiation that is manifest as a capacity to perform work (such as causing motion or the interaction of molecules)."

Another definition states, "a collision in which no energy is transferred."

An interesting definition, no? A collision in which no energy is transferred as if, in this great wide world of energy, no matter what *we do* ... our energy *just is*. It is not born, or destroyed, or called into formation from some dark place where it has been hiding.

Energy *just is* and because *it just is*, is in a constant state of motion.

It flows. It goes one direction, and comes back again. And so when we collide with that energy, the energy leading us to that collision *must have* been attracted to that collision, since no energy needed to be exchanged in order for us to get there in the first place.

All along, we are being pulled in a direction by energy which is always flowing, always moving, and always serving as a magnet. What type of magnet are we at this moment in time? And where is this magnet taking us?

And most importantly: how can we make sure that the direction of our magnet is moving toward that which we wish to attract?

* * *

TAKEAWAY TIP: Energy does not need to be created - only accessed. It is always present and it is always flowing. Therefore, we can choose to access positive energy at anytime, because it is always present around us. Everything we do is energy, and so with everything we do, we have the power to positively create.

* * *

Energy is Feeling

We can make sure that the direction of our magnet is positive by consciously raising our vibrational energy field to a place of positivity.

This is because energy is a feeling which attracts physical form in alignment *with* that feeling.

So if you are thinking positively about attracting money but you are feeling scared, desperate and concerned, you will not attract money. Sure, you may not attract more scarcity, but you certainly won't attract more money when you are vibrating in an energy space of fear.

But if you are thinking positively about money and also feeling positively about money - from spending it, to paying your bills, to waiting around patiently for more of it - then it will flow effortlessly to you.

mple and a fun shift for me regarding finances is this:

Negative energy around money:
"Ugh, I have to pay my rent again! I feel like I just did that!"

Positive energy around money:
"I am so blessed to be able to pay my rent, have this roof over my head and a fabulous apartment to welcome guests, family and friends. I am excited to pay this rent because it is a gift to me and my life!"

Your Thoughts Become Your Feelings

When a thought enters your mind and you're not sure why, the reason why is because your feelings are vibrating at a frequency equal to the frequency of that thought.

So even if you aren't trying to think negative thoughts, if you are feeling bad (sick, hurt, depressed, scared, powerless) your thoughts will naturally match this frequency.

Which is why self-motivation is rooted in self-talk. We must tell ourselves we are not the negative thoughts which come to us when we are in a tough spot. We must overcome the tough spot with a combination of new feelings and new thoughts.

A good question to ask yourself to more fully understand this concept is *"What do I effortlessly attract without even asking for it?"*

This can be good or bad attraction. In other words:

1. What people complain about becomes what they

continue to attract (and complain about).

2. What people celebrate becomes what they continue to attract (and celebrate).

In fact, let's take a few minutes to jot down in our Magic Manifestation journals what things we effortlessly attract.

Exercise #2
What Do You Effortlessly Attract — Good and Bad?

It's time to record what you effortlessly attract - both good *and* bad. Don't worry about writing down the bad, as you're simply acknowledging that these things show up. You're not sitting in the negative emotions associated with them, but rather taking an empowered stance to be a witness to them so that you may overcome and walk away from these blocks.

I'll share my list with you so you can get a gist of what to write in yours.

Sammy Effortlessly Attracts — What She Wants

1. Free clothing.
2. Invitations to stay at people's homes.
3. Friendships with new people and networking opportunities.
4. Collaboration opportunities for my business.
5. Free books.
6. Conversations with strangers.
7. Invitations to events.
8. Smiles and interaction with strangers on the street.

Sammy Effortlessly Attracts — What She Doesn't Want

1. Cuts and scrapes.
2. Being late.
3. Feeling overwhelmed
4. Emotionally unavailable dating partners.
5. Feeling like she's lost time.
6. Lack of focus within a certain period of time.
7. Tech issues.
8. Adding more onto her plate by saying "yes."

Now it's your turn!

What do you effortlessly attract which you do want:

_____

_____

_____

_____

_____

_____

_____

_____

_____

What do you effortlessly attract which you do not want:

_____

_____

_____

_____

_____

_____

_____

You may be loving your positive attraction list right now - and hating your negative attraction list.

Let go of hating the list. Because hating the list is only going to reinforce the energy which continues to attract those things. The negative attraction list is just as much an important part of you as the positive attraction list.

Rather, choose to practice shifting your energy and witnessing this negative attraction list as a fantastic opportunity to affirm what it is you really want.

Do I want to be late all of the time? No. So I affirm, *"I am always making time to be on time. I am commended for arriving early to all of my appointments."*

Do I want to feel like I'm always saying yes to things I don't want to do? No. So I affirm, *"I make the best decisions for me by responsibly weighing my options and making the most loving decision which aligns with my goals. I am in control of my schedule."*

So on and so forth.

Why Bad Things Happen to Good People

Everything you do, say, feel, think is energy. *Everything.*

Think about people in your life who say *'Why did this happen to me again, I can't believe this happened to me again!'*

The reason the bad circumstance or event happened to them again is because they continued to a.) complain about it b.) play victim to it c.) sit in the negative energy which attracted the negative event to them in the first place.

Just to show and prove to you just how simple it all really is, the equation that Albert Einstein came up with in 1924 to explain this "energy frequency thing" is E=MC2.

Sound complicated? As simple as this equation is, it may, until you know what E=MC2 means and what it stands for.

The e in Einstein's equation simply stands for energy and mc2 (mc "squared") is a really, really big number that represents what makes up 99.99999 percent of everything in the universe. So, in simplified terms it means that energy = everything. Well 99.99999 percent of everything, that is!

✳ ✳ ✳

> **TAKEAWAY TIP:** Because everything is energy and energy creates energy, remember that the most powerful tool you have on this planet is … you guessed it: your energy.

✳ ✳ ✳

The Levels of Energy

According to law of attraction experts Esther and Jerry Hicks and the teachings of Abraham, there are various degrees of energy feeling that we can be calibrating on in any given moment.

With greater self awareness of our energy level, we can understand what triggered us, how to positively exist within that space and how to, using various activities which best suit our style, *shift* out of a negative energy level and into a positive one.

Good feelings attract good things. Here are the various levels of "low vibration" (at the bottom) to high vibration (at the top) levels of emotion. A similar chart can be found in the book, "Ask and It Is Given," by Esther and Jerry Hicks, who communicate the tenets of law of attraction through Abraham, defined as "group consciousness from the non-physical dimension" according to the Esther and Jerry Hicks website.

HIGH (POSITIVE) VIBRATION

LEVEL 1
Joy, passion, empowerment, freedom, love, appreciation

LEVEL 2
Enthusiasm, eagerness, happiness, positive expectation, belief

LEVEL 3
Trust, optimism, hopefulness, contentment

LEVEL 4
Boredom, pessimism, frustration, irritation, impatience

LEVEL 5
Disappointment, doubt, worry, blame, discouragement, sadness

LEVEL 6
Anger, rage, revenge, hatred

LEVEL 7
Jealousy, insecurity, guilt, unworthiness

LEVEL 8
Fear, grief, depression, despair, powerlessness

LOW (NEGATIVE) VIBRATION

Exercise #3: What Energy Level Are You Right Now?

Take a moment to pause and reflect on what level you were calibrating at today.

Depending on the level, you were either calibrating on low vibration or high vibration. So even if you were thinking to yourself, *"I am attracting the job of my dreams,"* writing affirmations and speaking it into existence, if you were still in a place of feeling insecure or unworthy about this new job, you aren't calibrating at a vibration which would attract that job.

This is similar to how I described attracting abundance. If you ask for increased financial freedom but are feeling afraid of unpaid bills, rising expenses and the future of your life, you are blocking the flow of abundance to you. The channels aren't as clear as they could be.

Which is why for some things which we need to attract, it's not just about asking for it. It's about doing what we need to do to literally change our self-concept (Secret #1) and engage in other energy-shifting activities which allow us to feel energy at a high (i.e. positive) vibration surrounding the things we wish to attract and create in our lives.

The law of vibration, as it's called, states that everything in the universe vibrates. And as you learned, since everything is made up of energy (E=MC2) and energy has a vibration to it, that must mean everything has its own vibrational energy.

So, in order to attract something you want, then you must be at the same vibrational energy in order to attract it (like a magnet!) toward you.

The law of vibration states that *"Everything that is on the same vibrational frequency makes itself known to each other. When we send out signals on a certain frequency through our thoughts and emotions, the universe responds to us with anything and everything that resonates with that frequency."*

So, it is important that we learn to naturally *only* resonate with what we want versus resonate with what we are doubtful of, fearful of or insecure about. In other words: You reap what you sow, and what you put your attention to grows.

---

* * *

TAKEAWAY TIP: Be conscious of your energy level. Recognize that you can shift from one level to the next with your conscious decision to rise in vibration. Use this chart to note where you fall on the spectrum and set goals as to where you want to be. You've got the power.

* * *

All That Matters is Love

The most powerful emotion of all is ... *love*.

In fact, some law of attraction experts say that love is the "missing ingredient" to truly using all that the law of attraction has to offer. While love is grouped in level 1 on the emotional vibration chart by Esther & Jerry Hicks, it really deserves a level all its own, because love truly reigns supreme.

When love is your motivation, anything is possible. That's because love is everything categorized in level 1: freedom, joy, passion, empowerment, appreciation, etc.

So if you're doing something that you love, or believing in something that you love, or speaking about something that you love, then you're calibrating on that amazing vibrational energy! You have no need to even worry about the future behind your desires which are aligned in love: Because the highest and the best are coming to manifest themselves in this force field of love which *you* possess.

Oftentimes people have dreams they love, but they fear that they won't come true. So the fear overrides the love, because they're lacking trust behind their love. They feel the love but they don't trust they deserve to have the love. In essence, they feel *they don't deserve to pursue their dreams.*

When you've figured out what you love to do - and you know because you are feeling inspired, you are feeling empowered, you are feeling freedom, joy, passion, appreciation, gratitude, etc. - then all you need to do is just *go for it!*

There's a saying that "everything will work itself out." This is like the law of attraction working for you at exactly the right time and in exactly the right way. Your only focus is to trust your dreams and keep that love pure and not tainted with lower vibrational energy.

Some people aren't sure what they love. They're not sure what they want to attract, or what that's supposed to look like, or even feel like!

Which is why in my coaching I like to suggest that you go back to your passions as a child. What was it that you loved to do before you were about 10 years old? What did you naturally gravitate toward in your free time?

Whatever those activities were are signs of what you love (or will love) to do today.

* * *

TAKEAWAY TIP: Don't forget who you were as a child. That powerful, beautiful and special being had time to pursue passions without fear. The passions they participated with are signs of what you may wish to do and create for yourself today.

* * *

Following Your Love as a Child

There's a divine reason why I have considered myself a writer since I was 10 years old, when in the 5th grade I tested at the 9th grade reading level. Thanks to taking a course called fundamentals of journalism my sophomore year of high school, I was inspired to declare myself an aspiring journalist who wished to share other people's stories.

Today I am doing all of that and more - and while it didn't show up exactly as I had envisioned it for the long run, it did *show up*. I became a professional journalist, working for newspapers, lifestyle and trade magazines.

My first job out of college was as a web assistant for Esquire magazine.

I followed my inspiration and my dream showed up as I excitedly and lovingly pursued the path. I followed this whisper in my heart which, at a young age where I wasn't analyzing or trying to figure out everything I wanted to do with my life from a perspective of "doing what's safe,"

In other words, I didn't analyze what I wanted or chose "the safe path" of what promised financial support. No.

I wanted to be a writer, and so I simply pursued the call.

When I wanted to read, I read five books in one week. When I wanted to write, I jumped on my parents old, humming Gateway PC in 1995 and wrote short stories. I also used to imagine them in my head, or translate them into music for my clarinet.

You can probably look back to your childhood and notice how your interests are still a part of the things you wish to do today. You loved to play outside, and so now you make a point to go camping a few times a year. Or maybe you were always helping grandma in the kitchen, and currently you work in a bakery.

Or perhaps, you notice that your interests as a child are distinctly *not* a part of your life today. *At all!!*

And why might that be? Is it because you blocked yourself from following your love at a certain point in your young adulthood? Is it because you pursued a "safe path" that has drained your energy and leaves little time to pursue your interests?

Whatever the reason, if this scenario sounds like you, chances are you know when that moment happened, when you were given the option to choose *love* (i.e. continuing to listen to the inspiration) or choose *safety* (i.e. choose a major, an internship, a school, etc. which aligned with what felt safe for your financial security or reflected a cookie-cutter life path).

So when we realize what we love to do, who we love to be and what we love to see and feel, we can calibrate on the positive energy of these things and attract more of it into our life in full knowing that we are always being taken care of.

Sometimes we forget what we love to do or just need a reminder. This exercise gives you a chance to say hello to your

7-year-old self again. What did they love to do? If they could ask you to play right now, what would you they want you to play with them?

Exercise #4: 20 Things You Love to Do Now or Loved to Do Then

Imagine that you had a day of free time and it was infinite free time. What are 20 things you would do in this day which would make you happy?

Complete this exercise to jumpstart your "things-I-love-to-do list" so that you have knowledge as to the things you can do to keep you in that high vibrational place of *love*.

Here's my version for your inspiration!

1. Reading.
2. Listening to music.
3. Taking cool photos and pushing creative boundaries.
4. Exercising.
5. Drinking really good coffee.
6. Swimming.
7. Running in the forest.
8. Helping people one-on-one.
9. Thrifting and vintage shopping.
10. Playing dress-up and experimenting with makeup.
11. Coloring in coloring books
12. Free form journaling.
13. People watching.
14. Giving gifts.
15. Writing letters.
16. Going to museums.

17. Decorating.
18. Traveling and going on road trips.
19. Attending conferences and workshops.
20. Sitting in stillness on the beach.

Now it's your turn: Here's 20 lines, but feel free to expand!

_____
_____
_____
_____
_____
_____
_____
_____
_____
_____
_____
_____
_____
_____
_____
_____
_____
_____
_____
_____

* * *

TAKEAWAY TIP: See yourself doing more
of these things. Align your intention to do,
create, feel these things with love. The more you
participate in these activities you love doing, the
more you stay in high vibrational energy for life
itself.

* * *

The Other Secret to Love — It Overcomes All

It's not just about loving yourself or someone else, but loving every moment of your life. You get to literally ooze love with every meal you cook, every time you drive, whenever you answer the phone, walk into the office and see your boss is in a bad mood … *everything!*

I know it sounds impossible - to be in this state of absolute, 100 percent *love* literally all of the time, even when things are tough or seem to "happen to us" without warning.

Even when times are hard, we can choose to make the most of it by solving the problem, finding the solution and creating a peaceful situation from *a place of love*. Call it "finding the silver lining in the clouds" or "seeing the glass as half-full," but those clichés *are* clichés for a reason: *They work!*

Because yes, there will always be circumstances which require solution-finding. The path does have rocks and those rocks are there so that when walking, we can learn how to find the smoother and faster way next time we fall into the stride of life.

And to be in the best place to learn and live from our experiences using the tools of the law of the attraction is to be a witness to all experiences in our lives as situations which are here to serve and help (versus harm) us.

Rather than choosing to be a victim of a situation, we can choose to be a student of it. Rather than choosing to be down and out, we choose to be on the rise. Rather than choosing to be in a world which we do not enjoy, we are choosing to intentionally create our joy because we know best what makes us happiest.

We have the power to choose, the power to create, the power to connect with our highest vibrational selves. But so often we give it away to "forces unknown" we blame as culprits unfairly creating negative circumstances.

To love is a choice. No matter what circumstances may be at hand, you can choose to see the situation as a space to create more love and then from that place, allow positive energy to lead you the highest, best and brightest way.

What If You Have Fear?

And what if that fear is tainting your love so that no matter how much love you have for something, it's never going to attract what *you truly want?*

You may be asking yourself this question right now. Here's the answer: You can see your fear but not be your fear.

When a fearful thought rises your mind, you can choose to lovingly recognize it and compassionately release it.

Before understanding you had the power to choose love or choose fear, that fearful thought would sit with you and ruin your entire day, dream, desires and most importantly, spike that positive energy level *on down.*

If you want to stay in a place of fear, you have that choice too. But if you wish to stay at high vibration, you can see those fears and choose not to be those fears.

Note: This is not about fighting your fears, but flowing them out of your mind with love. It is perfectly natural for you to have these fear-based thoughts. We all do. Over time, they appear less and less … but they will still appear.

Here's a good example: Let's say you are looking for that job (flashback to Secret #1) and the belief *"I'm not good enough"* continually comes up for you.

This is your false belief that you aren't qualified for the jobs which you are applying for. *This is not true.* We have all seen people overcome their circumstances and prove themselves despite what may be "written on paper."

Rather than belittle yourself for having this belief that you aren't good enough to begin with, you can be happy that you now know it's there. Before you would have accepted these fear-based thoughts as true. Now, you see them as blocking your positive energy from prospering on your behalf and can actually do something about it.

Believing that you aren't enough is a false belief of yourself (Secret #1: change your self concept!) and now that you are blessed with the knowledge you are harboring this negative energy, you get to do whatever it takes to tell yourself and convince yourself just how qualified you actually are. *Because you are enough!*

Whether this is writing a love letter to yourself, jotting down a series of repetitive affirmations or speaking positively to yourself in the mirror every morning, you *can* shift out of this false belief so that it has less power over your thoughts, emotions and energy level.

Commit to seeing your fears and not being your fears by using positive self talk to change and redefine your self concept so that those fears are truly just laughable figments of your imagination.

Here are some examples of fearful thoughts which you can choose to see as - in the words of my favorite self development leader Gabby Bernstein - F.E.A.R. or, "false evidence appearing real."

I give you permission to see them as not real and not as a part of you. They are truly figments of your imagination.

1. I will never meet the partner of my dreams.
2. My parents don't think I've accomplished much with my life.
3. I am ridiculous for wanting what I do.
4. I don't deserve what it is that I want.
5. I'm not good enough for what it is that I want.
6. I'm making bad decisions with my life.

7. I'm disappointing people around me.
8. I'm not pretty enough.
9. I'm not confident enough.
10. I'm never going to have a life like "them."

* * *

TAKEAWAY TIP: Even when F.E.A.R. (false evidence appearing real) thoughts come up for you, you can smile and flick them away. *"Oh, you again!?"* you can think to yourself. *"I'm glad you stopped by ... but you're not welcome here."*

* * *

How to Stay in High Vibration (and Shift Your Energy)

Commit to doing this daily:

1. Exercising.
2. Getting enough sleep.
3. Meditating.
4. Playing a track of powerful, high energy music in the morning to dance and shake off any negative juju in your energy field.
5. Avoiding negative news.
6. Eating healthy food.
7. Smiling even when there's no reason to smile.
8. Practicing the vocalization, writing and celebration of gratitude for all the amazing things in your life.

Commit to using these tools to shift your energy when it is feeling low:

1. A good vibe tribe to talk to, text or call for a pick-me-up.
2. Writing a love letter to yourself.
3. Participating with visualization and guided meditations.
4. Writing affirmations.
5. Having conversations with yourself in the mirror.
6. Choosing to see the good in what you are "losing" as you know something more is on the way.
7. Looking at beautiful images.
8. Giving yourself a social media free day.

Not everyone stays committed to these daily activities, experiences and shifts. I, for one, don't always!

When I find myself in a place of funky negative juju, chances are I've been neglecting one of the eight daily activities outlined above. It could be lack of sleep, absorption of negative news, eating fried food and drinking too much wine, etc.

It's up to us to track of our behaviors so that they're in alignment with our goal to feel good and create good. Like taking care of your outer appearance, it's up to you to take care of your inner one, too.

Secret #3

Create *Consciously*

"Our goals can only be reached through a vehicle of a plan, in which we must fervently believe, and upon which we must vigorously act. There is no other route to success."
— Pablo Picasso

AFFIRMATION
My thoughts are my magnet. I can consciously attract whatever it is with thoughts rooted in expectation, love and purpose.

SONG
"The Power" — SNAP!

DEFINITION
Creation (noun): The act of making or producing something that did not exist before; Something new that is made or produced; Something that has been created; everything in the world.

IN THIS CHAPTER, WE WILL REVIEW:

1. The Power of Vision Boards
2. Why Your Desires Are Your Birthright
3. How to Create Your Own Vision Board
4. What to Put On Your Vision Board
5. The Importance of Being Specific
6. Seeing from the End of Your Life
7. Taking Abundant Action Now

Create Your Vision

I discovered the power of vision boards a few years ago and introduced the concept to a group of friends one New Year's Eve.

On December 30th, 2012, we mixed snacks, '90s music and a unique blend of fashion, fitness and business magazines into a pile before us to create a vision board making extravaganza that would prove to be one of the wisest investments of our time on this last day of the year.

Together we made our boards, enthusiastically cutting out images, words and declarations from the pages of magazines which inspired us.

We made massive piles of clippings by our sides. Some of us were more visually focused, while others cut inspirational headlines and subheads from articles.

Our vision boards were unique to us and, as the year would unfold, uniquely destined to create the vision we were looking to receive.

Friend Tammy Tibbetts and founder of She's the First, a non profit which enables girls to gain an education in disadvantaged countries, acknowledged her desire to increase donations for the year on her vision board.

As she was literally walking out the door, she checked her

email and saw what else? But an email saying she had received a $1,000 donation while literally making her vision board.

Tammy also chose to include a photo of Gloria Steinem on her vision board. She admired this leader's strength and her activism. She was certainly someone who showed up in the canon of inspirational women for Tammy.

Well, a few months later, Tammy was honored for She's the First as a winner of grant money from the Diane Von Furstenberg foundation.

She was asked to give a speech upon receiving the award. The speech was attended by an influential group of women including, none other than ... *Gloria Steinem.*

Tammy had the chance to meet Gloria backstage, even posing for a picture with her which she would later text me exclaiming, *"LOOK WHAT HAPPENED! Gloria was on my vision board!!!"*

I know. Get out of town right?!

And last, Tammy's vision board had a photo of Alicia Keys and in true vision board manifestation fashion, she ended up scoring free tickets to see Alicia perform in Central Park.

And that's not all - those are only the "crazy manifestations," as Tammy is a conscious creator by nature and saw her vision board as an opportunity to set goals. Every morning she woke up to see her vision board hanging on her wall, a reminder of what she wanted to focus on and create for the year 2013.

My vision board? It more than "came true," it was a catalyst for my creation of it. The unexpected - like Tammy's experiences - did occur. I purchased a new computer (there was a photo of a laptop on the board), I appeared on TV two distinct times (there was a photo of a woman in a TV), and I gained spiritual wisdom and expansion when I was unexpectedly asked to join a self development program in Los Angeles toward the end of 2013.

But there's more! I won't dive into the details of my conscious creation - because I want you to get ready (and revved!) for yours.

Born to be a Conscious Creator — Your Desires Are Your Birthright

Before I jump into vision board making and how to use them to consciously create …

Let's go back to exercise #4 in Secret #2, because I want to remind you that your desires are your birthright.

Remember what you wrote on your list of things you loved to do as a child? Chances are that list includes things which you remain attracted to today.

The things you loved to do as a child are indicators of what strengths, talents and potential accolades were given to you by a higher power.

Therefore, your desires aren't necessarily what *you* created for *you*.

Your desires are what you were *born to have without you having to do a single thing to attract them.* You simply wanted what it was that you were led to do. There was a call. There was a yearning. Perhaps, there was even a pain if this yearning wasn't fulfilled.

Many spiritual seekers credit their talents *to* God. They simply thank God for giving them their talents.

You can give credit to whichever source shows up as relatable for you - be it your God, the universe, spirits, angels, heaven, etc. - but recognize that, since you were given these desires at such a young age when very little of life's opportunities had left an impression on you, well, there must be a uniquely divine reason why you prefer coloring in color books and making pots from clay versus riding motorcycles over dirt hills or jumping out of airplanes. *Get it?*

Listening to your heart, therefore, is your divine right. It is a right you were born with and which intuitively, you know is true for you.

Which is why Secret #3 is not just about lining up your emotions to harmonize with positive thoughts to positively create what you want to see emerge in your life, but to also tap into what you *truly* want in your life.

* * *

TAKEAWAY TIP: The law of attraction works like a radio signal: the sharper and clearer it is, the more responsive the energy can be. But when our desires are confused or unclear? We're giving off mixed signals and can expect to receive mixed results in return. Be as specific as possible, and do whatever it takes to learn what exactly you want those specifics to be.

* * *

Vision Boards — Creating What You Wish to Be, Do & Have

Vision boards help to create a clear signal to the universe as to what we wish to create, manifest and attract into our lives.

A vision board is a piece of paper - any size - which is a visual rendition of what you are looking to create in your life. Most vision board makers use magazines, scissors and glue to illustrate their hopes, dreams and desires; but sketching, writing and even using symbols works just the same so long as your energetic vibration is in a place of excitement and enthusiasm for what it is you are illustrating.

In other words, what matters most is how you feel about your vision board. Does it make you excited for your life's potential? Then you are creating, declaring and manifesting your vision through the power of conscious creation.

Vision boards are powerful tools for goal setting and manifestation making. *Think and Grow Rich* author Napoleon Hill famously said: *"Plan your plan and work your plan."*

And that's exactly why vision boards are so powerful. They are your visual plan displaying what you will energetically focus on for the year, half year or within seasonal increments.

What You Need to Make a Vision Board

- Scissors

- Rubber cement. Key note: Not generic white Elmer's glue! Use *rubber* cement!

- Magazines representing various disciples. Key note: Don't just use fashion magazines because you won't find a variety of images to represent your "circle of life," as explained in the pages ahead.

- Extra large poster board, as if you were presenting at a science fair.

- Positive tunes to play while in the midst of creation. I recommend turning up these jams from my site: sammyd.tv/positive-playlist.

- Girlfriends and boyfriends joining to create a vision board making party. Present your vision boards at the end so that you can begin to speak them into existence before an audience.

- My smile, support and belief in you! In episode #12 of *SAMMYD TV, I share how to make a vision board and the reasons you should do it. Watch the episode on my site: sammyd.tv/vision-boards-ep12.

<u>Be Specific. Create Specific. Attract Specific.</u>

What do you need that's more important than the tools?

You need to know exactly what it is you wish to manifest.

This can be difficult for someone who has never sat down to consciously create. Perhaps you've just let life "happen to you," versus thinking deep as to what you want and taking a stand for that … and that only.

Remember the exercise from Secret #2 about what you loved doing as a child? Let's return to that and re-read your answers in your Magic Manifestation journal.

Didn't do it? *Nudge, nudge.* It's time to do it.

Because after we've acknowledged what it is we loved doing as children, we can begin to feel what it is we want as adults.

Whatever it is was that you loved doing as a child, loved feeling as a child, loved thinking about as a child, is a reflection of your inherent right manifested in the early years of your life, before the world began to tell you "no" and you believed it.

The reason reflecting on your childhood passions is because this was the time when you thought anything was possible. You hadn't yet met the world's restrictions, boundaries and expectations.

When making your vision board, you want to tap into your childhood optimism for life. Pretend you are 7 years old again: You *can* choose to erase the world's beliefs for you. This vision board is your blank canvas, and you get to create whatever it is you truly wish.

Your Life Purpose

After flipping back to your answers from exercise #4 of Secret #2, you have a foundation to draft your life purpose, which by now you've realized will help give insights to consciously create the vision board of your *authentic*, awesome dreams.
Your childhood passions should give you clues - and provoke memories - of who you truly are and love to do. Even if you haven't done it since you *were* a child!

Back to your life purpose: Understanding your life purpose can help you to understand how to use the law of attraction to consciously create whatever it is that you want.

But so many people are uncertain as to exactly what their life purpose is. I ask them this question and a look of confusion crosses their faces, and they tilt their heads as if to say, *'Huh?'*

That's why it's important to take time to do the following exercises so that you can begin to calibrate on an energy of creation which is aligned with *who you truly are* and *what you truly want.*

Again: Not what the world has told you is safe and practical.

Rather, you want to dig deep and listen to your heart. Because when you know who you are and what you want, the confusion surrounding decisions lessens. You trust more. Good things happen to you effortlessly. When you follow your heart because you know what your heart wants, the path is easily laid before you.

Life becomes easier when you know what you want because you have decided and declared who you're out to be and what you're out to create in the world. In other words, the laws of the universe work in your favor, which is why you have no fear asking, trusting, and receiving. The law of attraction has taught you that your specific desires are always on the way.

But if you don't know what to ask for, you're certainly never going to receive. Which is why the next exercise is going to prove truly invaluable for you.

Exercise #1: The Circle of Life

To complete this exercise, give yourself 45 minutes to write what you want in each slice of the pie in the "Circle of Life."

Each category below represents a different slice from the pie that is the Circle of Life.

Work
Play
Finances
Relationships
Family
Stress Mastery
Exercise
Diet
Spirit
Self Esteem
Life Purpose
Environment - Home
Health
Self-Care

Take a look at each category, and write down a few things you want in each for the rest of your life.

If you could consistently thrive in these areas in specific ways, what would you want from this moment forward?

Tip #1: When writing out your answers to this exercise, refrain from using words like *'want to'* or *'I'd like to'* or *'I wish that.'* Speak in the affirmative. We'll get more to this in Secret #6.

Tip #2: When writing out your answers to this exercise, refrain from just including mentions of the good you *already* have. This is about expanding beyond what you have now, assuming you're looking to break free of the boundaries you may have set for yourself previously. Go beyond your plate now and add some new dishes to the beautiful platter you already have before you.

Allow yourself to free form write until the most radical and emotionally charged ideas emerge. It may be slow at first which is why you must keep writing even if you don't know what to write at first. You'll know that something is powerful when you laugh, cry, smile or just feel a surge of energy through your body upon writing it down. Listen to that emotion.

If this exercise requires more space, start here and add additional pieces of paper to expand your answers.

What You Want in ... Work

_____
_____
_____
_____
_____
_____
_____
_____

What You Want in ... Play

_____
_____
_____
_____
_____
_____
_____

What You Want in … Finances

_____
_____
_____
_____
_____
_____
_____

What You Want in … Relationships

_____
_____
_____
_____
_____
_____

What You Want in … Family

_____
_____
_____
_____
_____
_____
_____

What You Want in … Stress Mastery

_____
_____
_____
_____
_____
_____

What You Want in ... Exercise

_____

_____

_____

_____

_____

_____

_____

_____

What You Want in ... Diet

_____

_____

_____

_____

_____

_____

_____

_____

What You Want in ... Spirit

_____

_____

_____

_____

_____

_____

_____

_____

What You Want in ... Self Esteem

_____

_____

_____

_____

_____
_____
_____
_____

What You Want in ... Life Purpose

_____
_____
_____
_____
_____
_____
_____

What You Want in ... Environment/Home

_____
_____
_____
_____
_____
_____
_____

What You Want in ... Health

_____
_____
_____
_____
_____
_____
_____

What You Want in ... Self Care

_____

_____

_____

_____

_____

_____

_____

_____

* * *

TAKEAWAY TIP: This exercise shows
how you cannot know what you want in
all areas of your life until you *consciously
write it out*. There is no way you can
properly answer these questions if I
were to ask you them on the spot. The
time this exercise requires is worth it.

* * *

Imagine if I were to stop you on the street and say, '*So, what
are you goals for life in the area of self-care?*' Perhaps you'd have an
answer after a few minutes of mental debate, but the real truth
is revealed when you take the time to sit and truly spell out your
highest desires. Give it time, and the answers will come.

_____

Manifestation Power Punch

After handwriting your responses to what you want related to each slice from the circle of life, type it out. Type it out so that you can print multiple copies and place them in spots where you can deliberately or accidentally pull them out to casually read as a regular reminder of *what you are on this planet to do, be and attract.*

I have a list of life goals in my wallet at all times. I also have a list of the qualities I am attracting in the love of my life - my co-creator, fellow life walker, forever life partner. I've also kept affirmations, love letters to myself and other motivational messages within reach so that when the moment strikes, they're waiting to lift me higher and remind me of the miracle that is my life.

I love pulling out these memories of manifestation. They not only bring a smile to my face, but re-center my energy to the levels they were when I first wrote them. And when we return to the state of positive energy which is harmonious alignment with what we wish to create, we are using that "like" energy to attract the "like" energy associated with what we are optimistically looking to create.

* * *

TAKEAWAY TIP: There is nothing you cannot do. You simply must stay in the belief that it is possible for you. That is your only responsibility.

* * *

Commit Before You're Ready

In order for the law of attraction to truly work on your behalf, you must be willing to put in the work when opportunity knocks.

You can attract opportunities, connections, requests, e-mails, phone calls, door bells ringing and chance encounters, but if you don't take action when the universe answers your attraction calibration, then that energy will keep flowing - *past you!* - because you failed to take action to bottle it up and create something with it.

Remember the classic definition of energy? Merriam Webster defines it as, *"The capacity for vigorous activity"* and also *"An adequate or abundant amount of such power."*

So if you receive the energy you were looking to attract but do not use the energy when you receive it, it will keep moving because it is a free flowing source of the universe which cannot create anything until its receiver chooses to use it.

Which is why sometimes people joke that *'The universe has been showing me signs,'* yet nothing happens from those signs because they've been choosing to ignore them by not taking action. Eventually, the signs will dissipate if you choose to ignore them.

In lesser words: Don't delay jumping into the energy you are receiving. And in more words: Begin to take action to attract what it is you want *now*.

When you take action, your energy shifts to a place of commitment. Your energy is ripe for creation and because of your already confident action, you receive more energy needed to create. The river of attraction and action starts flowing, and it won't stop!

So if you want to pursue a job in the public arts, why not start a blog about the murals in your city?

If you want to meet the love of your life, why not treat yourself like the love of your life?

If you want to be on TV, why not start your own YouTube channel?

Yes, these are simple ideas that you may or may not be able to do. But chances are you *can* do them. You simply have to choose to prioritize.

And if you want to do more but can't do more (i.e. you want to be on Broadway but moving to New York City is financially not an option right now) do what you can with what you have now, and calibrate on the energy that you are receiving the financial freedom you need to hit the streets of New York City like the star under the lights you truly are.

Exercise #3: Take Abundant Action Now

If you have blocks against taking action, it's time for you to plan how you can take small steps *now*.

There is always *something* you can do. If you say *'There's nothing I can do to pursue my goals,'* then you are creating a pretty firm block against the law of attraction working on your behalf, because you are saying that you are incapable of creating with the energy you want to come your way.

And again: That energy *wants* to be used!

Write answers to the following statements to begin planning how you can take small steps to begin pursuing the goals you wish to create, manifest and attract into completion.

YOUR GOAL: *I want to …*

_____

_____

_____

_____

_____

_____

_____

YOUR CONNECTIONS: *I can speak to …*

_____

_____

_____

_____

_____

_____

_____

YOUR EDUCATION: *I can learn about ....*

_____

_____

_____

_____

_____

_____

YOUR ONE SMALL ACTION: *I can commit to ...*

_____

_____

_____

_____

_____

_____

YOUR GROWTH: *I can do more of ....*

_____

_____

_____

_____

_____

_____

Try this exercise for at least one thing you want to attract, and you'll be revealed the steps of action you can take *now* which will sharpen your radio signal to attract the energy you need to fulfill your dreams.

To truly be a conscious creator, we must commit before we are ready.

The little ego voice (or your "nerds," "the committee," "your dark side," etc.) will tell you that you're *never ready*. It will tell you that you're *never good enough*. It will tell you that the world thinks *ill of you for pursuing what it is you want.*

It will also tell you that *you're just fine where you are* - why do you need more? Why aren't you satisfied with what you've got?

NONE OF THIS IS TRUE.

The secret to letting go of these ego-driven thoughts of scarcity, unworthiness and thinking small is to remember that you were born a creator.

In a religious sense, you were born as an image of God who is your creator. You are a reflection of Him, and therefore create in his name (refer back to Secret #2 for all the inspiration you need on why you were born a creator).

So to talk yourself *out* of that negative self talk is the key to staying on task and believing that you deserve to stay on task.

Which, you do.

Look at this action-activation activity as something which strengthens your attraction signal - as if your actions are radar alerts activating a center just ready to explode on your behalf.

And look out! Because once that energy center is activated, you're going to get *a lot* coming your way!

Secret #4

Declare Abundance & Affirm It's *Already Here*

"You get whatever accomplishment you are willing to declare."
— Georgia O'Keeffe

AFFIRMATION
I am a crazy creator of opportunity today.

SONG
"Make Yourself" — Incubus

DEFINITION
Declaration (noun): The act of declaring; announcement; a declaration of dividend; A positive; explicit; or formal statement; proclamation; Something that is announced; avowed, or proclaimed.

IN THIS CHAPTER, WE WILL REVIEW:

1. My Decision to be Free
2. The Power of Your Tongue
3. How to Write & When to Use Affirmations
4. Why Affirmations Can Positively Shift a Situation
5. Resources for Writing Affirmations
6. Thinking Bigger Than You Think

The Day I Became a Free Bird

Five years ago I was sitting at the desk of my corporate magazine job when I began to hear a little voice.

That little voice told me that I was destined for something. Something bigger. Something bolder, braver and beyond anything I had ever imagined up to that point at age 23.

It was then that I launched a clothing brand called Sammy Davis Vintage as the modern women's vintage boutique for trends and styles contemporary for today.

I began selling at flea markets and door-to-door. I hosted pop-up shops at friend's apartments. I even opened a boutique of my own in the storage unit of a Manhattan Mini Storage Unit on the Upper East Side.

I began to see myself as someone spreading the joys of vintage fashion to cool, trendy 20-something girls.

But I was still working my full time job as a web assistant for a prominent magazine. And I still wasn't *all* happy. From Monday to Friday I worked at a desk and stared at a computer for eight hours a day. I felt like there was a ball and chain shackling my feet to that desk.

It got so bad that every time I would put on my favorite Crosby, Stills, Nash & Young song, I would begin to cry. Tears would bubble up to my eyelids and because I was sitting on the

24th floor of one of the most powerful publishing companies in the world, I would have to suppress them so that no one would see.

And that just made them hurt more - because they weren't being released.

A week after reading Gary Varynucks book, *Crush It* (released in 2008 and now considered classic text behind creating your digital own brand), I came home from the magazine office and told my roommate, *'I'm quitting my job on Friday.'*

The day I quit my job, I felt like I was going to vomit. I can remember Google chatting with a friend, telling her that I was about to get sick but I was going to do it anyway. I had to. I had to do something different to step on a different path which fulfilled my soul.

And what was it that I wanted which would fulfill my soul? As inspired by Gary's book, I wanted to create the Internet's largest vintage fashion destination online.

I wanted to be the #1 site for vintage fashion, sharing everything about styles of the past with anyone who wanted to learn. I also, as inspired by Gary's book, wanted to focus on producing video. I wanted to be on camera, smiling, laughing and spreading the joys of vintage fashion via digital film, using portals like YouTube to spread my message around the world.

A few days after I put in my two weeks notice, I sat down for lunch with my soon-to-be ex boss and declared to him my intentions.

I told him that I wanted to launch the *"digital destination for vintage fashion"* and create a content hub *"focused on video."*

Flash forward approximately a year after quitting that job.

I was not only working with two other women on producing a pilot about food, fashion and music across America called "Road Hug," but I had begun posting videos on positive thinking and sharing them with my rising social media audience after founding Sammydvintage.com, the site for modern woman who loved to wear, love and learn about vintage fashion.

In a nutshell, I was taking action and successfully attracting the elements I needed to make my dream a reality.

But something was missing: A business partner.

I wanted to grow my video presence so that it was reaching more people, and I wanted to do it professionally.

In my storage unit on the Upper East Side where I sold vintage clothes, I can remember saying to a friend: *'I would like to have a business partner.'*

September 2010, I received an email from a man who had graduated film school, previously worked as a digital video producer and was looking to create a YouTube channel in a niche category like vintage fashion.

He asked me if I'd be interested in meeting, as he had found my blog searching for vintage fashion bloggers on Google.

Basically, reader, this man was proposing to me *exactly* what I had declared, what I had desired and what I had been manifesting for nearly a year.

I met him in Bryant Park and within two weeks, we had decided to form a partnership to grow Sammy Davis Vintage as the go-to destination for inspiring videos and content on vintage fashion.

The YouTube channel, website and social media platforms became so successful that I went on to not only manage one of New York City's trendiest vintage boutiques in the Lower East Side, gain 20,000 subscribers to my YouTube channel and write a best selling eBook called *The 100 Best Vintage Shops Online*, but I also spoke to numerous production companies about reality TV show ideas and was eventually cast for *Thrift Wars*, a show initially scheduled to air on Oxygen in spring 2013.

The reality show never aired because after filming the pilot, Oxygen pulled the plug. Thankfully so, because it would have been a sour moment for my brand, which was rooted in positivity, love and creative self expression. The show? You could say it was *very little of that.*

But here I am writing to you, having consciously created what I had set out to do at age 23 when I left my safe and secure corporate publishing job.

Quitting your day job may not be for you, but my heart knew that safe path wasn't for me. And when those tears wouldn't stop running down my cheeks as I sat miserably behind my desk, I decided to decide that in taking that leap of faith, the parachute for safety would come.

And float down from the airplane I certainly did - and am still doing today.

I share this story with you because I've lived the journey of manifestation.

But I've also lived the journey of self doubt, second guessing, worry, fear, anxiety and questioning my path.

What I've learned in the five years as my own boss is that it all works out and that *"The universe always has your back."*

Declare What You Wish to Consciously Create

From the moment I declared, *'I want to have the online destination for vintage fashion'* to my boss, I was telling the universe with my enthusiastic energy what it was I wished to attract.

I was 100 percent focused in my intention as to what I wanted to specifically create next.

I was also asking for a realistic expectation that I was excited to create and passionately believed could happen for me, because I had read Gary Vaynerchuk's *Crush It* which had the motivational information which stated I could with tips on how to do it.

When you've decided what it is you wish to consciously create as I had with Sammy Davis Vintage, begin to talk the walk to everyone you meet.

When I was manifesting the arrival of my business partner, I was talking the talk. I was telling people that I wanted a business partner. I was telling people that the next step to Sammy Davis Vintage was having a business partner. I was explaining to them that in order to build the brand I wanted to build, that a business partner was desired, if not absolutely necessary.

What is it that you're looking to create in your life, and how can you go about talking the walk to everyone you meet?

Exercise #1: Talk the Talk

You don't have to sound crazy when you're talking the talk. Here's a few suggestions for having healthy conversations with people about what you want to create. And trust me when I say this: What you say will inspire them to begin thinking about what it is they're out to consciously create, too.

Tip #1: Create a mastermind group. Bring together a group of friends once a week to talk about how they are pursuing their goals, what they are looking to create and how they are abundant.

Use a conference call line and set a regular time to check in. Give each other five to 10 minute shares (limit the group to no more than five people, intimacy is always better for reciprocated communication) and use this weekly call to not only check in and keep tabs on one another's progress, but to speak whatever it is you wish to create into existence and have a platform to share with people who will give you positive feedback that *'Yes! You are able to create whatever it is you wish.'*

Tip #2: Talk to yourself in the mirror. This may seem very Rocky-esque of me to suggest, but there's a reason it works for athletes - and it will work for you, too. All you need to do is stand in front of a mirror and talk to yourself as if you were talking to a friend telling them what it is you are creating.

You may feel awkward at first, but as your comfort level increases so will the confidence in your voice and self expression. And that confidence? It'll set the wheels in motion for positive energy and positive attraction to flow through your veins. I promise you'll literally feel a surge of good juju emanate from your body after completing this portion of the exercise.

The person you need to persuade the most is yourself. Truly, once you persuade and actualize the belief in yourself, you won't fear communicating what it is you're out to create to others.

Example goal: *'I want to be a TV show host, a documentary filmmaker and a leader of change through media.'*

So to instill the belief that I deserve to be and do this, I would speak to myself as such:

'Hey Sammy! It's good to see you! So the latest with me is I'm really feeling good about attracting opportunities to be on TV. I have this dream to have a cross country road trip TV show where I visit vintage festivals, shows, historic homes, diners, drive-ins, collectors, and never before seen destinations to spread the joy of vintage love to the world! I want to be on the cover of magazines as the girl who made history hot, I want to be in the social circles of celebrities and singers/songwriters of Los Angeles, I want to be the owner of product lines and a motivational speaker at events for causes I believe in.

I want to have the influence and wealth to give back and create what I love. I want to be an artist recognized for her gifts and working with other people who push my creative limits and challenge me to greatness.

I want to be known in the cultural canon of entertainers, influencers and creators. I want to be famous. I want to be remembered. I want to leave a dent on the world.'

Admittedly, reader, it felt awkward writing that. My little ego voice was telling me as I wrote it that there's *no way* that is going to happen!

Be practical! Be logical! It was telling me. *'You?! A TV show host? You? Famous? You, known in the world? You're 28 years old - let go of that pipe dream, girl!'*

That little ego voice will come up as you speak to yourself. But we get to remember our power and use that memory to shut it down. We can choose to see it, but not *be it*.

Tip #3: Find someone who has done what you want to do and ask if you can speak to them about what you wish to create. This doesn't just have to be a business owner or someone in a position of power or success. This could be someone who seems truly happy, or has a healthy relationship, or lost 100 pounds with exercise and diet.

Or perhaps you're looking to have less stress in your life and want to learn how to do it. Who on your Facebook feed always seems to be chill, going with the flow and emanating good energy? Facebook message them, compliment what it is they have which you want, and ask them for advice. They'll be so flattered you asked, that they'll happily share their secrets with you.

Tip #4: Let go of caring what people think about you. Are you doubting your own dreams and vocalization of them to the world?

If the answer is even a tiny but yes, chances are you're concerned with one of the following:

1. **The expectations of others** and what they believe is *safe* and *good* for you, whether based on their own personal experiences or looking at your own past history as a record book for them to reference.
2. **Your self image.** What if you fail? What if you can't do it? What will the world think, after you told the world you were set to create this one thing and then *voosh!* It wasn't created? But then again, what if you *didn't try at all?*
3. **Their reaction.** Sure, not everyone is going to support you. Sure, there are going to be naysayers. But by sharing your dream with them, you just might plant a glimmer of hope in their hearts about the fact that *they too* can create what they want in the world. It's not just about you when you share your dreams - it's about them, too.

Letting go of caring what other people think about you is perhaps the most useful tip I can offer to give you the confidence to speak your hopes and dreams into existence.

Leaders speak their hopes and dreams into existence no matter the naysayers, the feedback or the present reality.

Here's a few examples:

- Martin Luther King, Jr.
- Gloria Steinem
- Susan B. Anthony
- Mahatma Ghandi
- Abraham Lincoln
- Mother Teresa
- Nelson Mandela
- Thomas Edison
- Bill Gate
- Steve Jobs
- Rosa Parks
- [insert your favorite historical leader here]

If the members of this list had chosen not to see, speak and take action toward the vision they had but which wasn't yet apparent in the world, we wouldn't have had the radical, empowering and liberating change they created to better the lives of *all*.

* * *

TAKEAWAY TIP: A conscious creator is someone who has vision where there is no reason to see what they are seeing. Be an

inspirational leader in your own life - speak
what you desire to create into existence, not just
because you want it but *because the world needs it.*

* * *

The Power of Affirmations

*"Grateful souls focus on the happiness and abundance present in their
lives and this in turn attracts more abundance and joy towards them."*
— Stephen Richards, *Think Your way to Success: Let Your Dreams
Run Free*

I couldn't have said it better myself.

Affirmations are the most powerful tool that you can access
anywhere you happen to be. Writing affirmations everyday
keeps you in a place of gratitude and grounds you into the
moment that is always more powerful than you think.
When we write affirmations daily, we access our feel-good
source of positivity that triggers all positive thoughts,
encounters and events to effortlessly enter our lives.

This is because the law of attraction is rooted in the power
of affirmative belief. Because when we begin to focus on the
positive, we begin to calibrate on the energy of the positive,
and therefore as the laws of the universe dictate and which
was described in Secret #1, we begin to *attract* more positive as
a result of *focusing* only on the positive.

Affirmations work because they align and center our energy only in the good.

Defined as *"The action or process of affirming something or being affirmed,"* affirmations are declarations and statements that serve as positive anchorings to empower our minds, hearts and energy.

In other words: They make us feel good and with repetition, can re-wire our brains and permanently change our perception of ourselves and what we can create in the world.

Additionally, repeating positive words and phrases is a proven psychological self-help process for changing, adding or removing specific behaviors and habits.

In the words of affirmation queen Louise Hay, founder of Hay House publishing company, *"You are the only person who thinks in your mind! You are the power and authority in your world."*

So often we think that the world is happening *to* us. But it is truly happening as a result of who we are being *in that moment.*

Which is why I suggest that affirmations be used for creating the good, and for strengthening our power beyond the bad.

When we have circumstances which feel beyond our control, how would we prefer handling them?

Option A: With a victim mentality that achieves very little toward a solution or at best, finds a solution with self-inflicted pain and suffering?

Option B: With a successful attitude that is optimistic a solution is within sight, and which fuels the path with good energy toward finding that solution because it *is possible* with persistence and perseverance?

The latter sounds much better, much less painful and certainly, no matter the good or bad circumstances *now,* living life to the fullest.

Writing, speaking, thinking and sharing affirmations can help us to stay positive so that no matter what is happening, we are creating positive results in the present moment.

Because life is now, and right now is all that matters.

Exercise #2: Writing Affirmations Daily

Every morning I write.

A daily devotion to writing is what sets apart the dreamers from the doers, because it is when we begin to write that we gain momentum to do.

Scholars, writers, artists and prominent men and women in America will all agree: A daily writing practice is a spiritual practice of finding, feeling and activating our inherent strength within.

This strength I speak of is always present, but it's up to us to remember to *choose* that it's there so that we can consciously access it.

I suggest writing the following to structure your affirmation writing exercise. Let's begin harnessing the power of affirmation writing for you right now, shall we?

1. I am *creating* ... _____

2. I am *attracting* ..._____

3. I am *believing* ..._____

4. I am *being* ... _____

5. I am *leading* ..._____

6. I am *sharing* ..._____

7. I am *trusting* ..._____

8. I am *honoring* ..._____

9. I am *inspiring* ... _____

10. I am *empowering* ... _____

Other activating words you can use to set up your affirmations are the following, but I suggest using the first 10 regularly and then add additional affirmations as feels appropriate for you.

1. I am *celebrating* ..._____

2. I am *loving* ... _____

3. I am *giving* … _____

4. I am *helping* … _____

5. I am *allowing* … _____

6. I am *asking* … _____

7. I am *forgiving* … _____

8. I am *solving* … _____

9. I am *improving* … _____

10. I am *growing* … _____

11. I am *learning* … _____

For energizing inspiration on how to write affirmations, watch episode #2 of *SAMMYD TV for a video tutorial on how to write affirmations on my site: sammyd.tv/video-write-affirmations-feel-good.

In my coaching I've learned that people struggle to find positive words to describe how they wish to feel (and that's totally OK!).

Which is why I've listed 101 positive words for positive thinking and positive affirmation writing - keep this list handy!

101 Positive Words for Affirmation Writing

1.	abundance	29.	exciting
2.	amazing	30.	exquisite
3.	approved	31.	fabulous
4.	attractive	32.	fantastic
5.	beaming	33.	faith
6.	beautiful	34.	flourishing
7.	bliss	35.	fortunate
8.	brave	36.	free
9.	brilliant	37.	fresh
10.	calm	38.	friendly
11.	celebrated	39.	fun
12.	certain	40.	giving
13.	courageous	41.	glamorous
14.	content	42.	glowing
15.	complete	43.	good
16.	creative	44.	gorgeous
17.	delightful	45.	graceful
18.	divine	46.	great
19.	ecstatic	47.	happy
20.	efficient	48.	healthy
21.	effortless	49.	heavenly
22.	electrifying	50.	honored
23.	elegant	51.	independent
24.	enchanting	52.	intuitive
25.	encouraging	53.	intelligent
26.	energized	54.	joy
27.	engaging	55.	jubilant
28.	enthusiastic	56.	kind

57. knowing
58. light
59. love
60. miraculous
61. motivated
62. nurturing
63. one-hundred percent
64. open
65. optimistic
66. paradise
67. perfect
68. peace
69. positive
70. powerful
71. prepared
72. pretty
73. productive
74. progress
75. protected
76. proud
77. ready
78. respected
79. rewarded
80. safe
81. secure
82. sparkling
83. special
84. stunning
85. strong
86. successful
87. supported
88. thrilling
89. thriving
90. tranquil
91. transforming
92. trusting
93. unwavering
94. upbeat
95. valued
96. vibrant
97. victorious
98. vivacious
99. wealthy
100. whole
101. worthy

* * *

TAKEAWAY TIP: You are more powerful
than you think, and writing affirmations
everyday will, with each new dawn, affirm
your strength to choose your thoughts, choose

your life, and choose actions toward positive creation, change and commitment to peaceful solutions for any circumstance at hand.

* * *

How Affirmations Can Help to Let Go of Negative Beliefs

When I first stepped on the path of spiritual self-discovery, writing affirmations was my most beloved tool of healing.

It was with affirmations that I could let go of the negative beliefs I was holding on to. I was holding on to limiting beliefs, past experiences and future fears that ultimately, were doing absolutely *nothing* to serve me in the moment.

And as I wrote, the tears flowed and a peaceful serenity came over me. Each affirmation writing session was like a self-led therapy session which allowed me to focus, feel and serve the good in my life from a place of peace and inner-knowing that everything was going to work out.

While writing affirmations, an emotional release may show up for you. I wanted to address this before moving forward because if you have yet to dig up the wounds of the past or perhaps acknowledge the self-inflicted pain you're placing on yourself now, the negative juju you've been holding on to may bubble to the surface, and *fast.*

And if, like me, you were pushing it down as if it didn't exist, when it breaks ground there *will* be pain.

One of the most beloved phrases of the self development industry is to *"trust the process."* So if this scenario becomes similar to your own affirmation writing experience, I leave with you the three words: Trust the process.

Where to Put Affirmations

Affirmations are tools to help elevate our energy so that it returns to an energetically positive place of great love, expectation and optimism for our lives, which we can choose to believe are always attracting what we need for our highest good.

I have literally have affirmations placed all around my two bedroom Manhattan apartment. They are conveniently hung so that at any point in the day, I can re-read them (for the upteenth time!) and *remember* the positive feeling, *feel* the positive feeling and *vibrate* on the positive feeling they promote.

Here are some easy spots in the home, office and your own personal space to place affirmations. There's no excuse not to use some of this real estate to surround yourself with the good juju affirmations inspire us to feel.

Places to Position Affirmations

1. Your refrigerator door.
2. A bulletin board.

3. Your bedside, such as in a picture frame.
4. In your wallet.
5. As a canvas print hanging on your bedroom wall (check out Staples to convert photos into canvas prints, or my collection of Lipstick Affirmations prints on Society6: society6.com/sammydstyle).
6. On your mirror using Post-It notes.
7. At your work desk, especially if you have a bulletin board in a cubicle where you can pin things.
8. On the dashboard of your car.
9. In the pages of a book you are reading, a printed agenda, or as the desktop background on your computer or iPhone.
10. On the desktop of your computer or smart phone background.

I literally have notebooks overflowing with affirmations, letters to myself and exercises I've done.

When I open one of these books and re-remember what it is I found to be true within myself the moment I wrote it, I feel great comfort and am reminded of whatever the message was for me in that moment.

Affirmations return us to positive energy *again*, and *again* and *again*. There's nothing wrong with continually needing to remind yourself to vibrate on the good, either. I constantly remind myself to vibrate on it, which is why I am so successful at it!

The same can be said of a workout routine: You can't just workout for a few weeks and then expect to have that body forever.

If you stop working out, over time you will lose the body and will eventually need to start from scratch. So rather than stop working out completely, lose it all and have to start fresh, you can continue to workout to maintain it and know that your strength is always accessible for you.

So, affirmations are a beautiful tool to maintain the feelings you wish to have consistently over time. And they are a simple way to remind yourself of the path you know is best to stay on: The path of positive thinking, feeling and creating.

How & When to Use Affirmations

The placement of affirmations in strategic places around your home will help to make positive thinking, shifting and actualizing a 24/7 thing for you.

In your life, there will be moments when the power of affirmations can not only help you to positively create, but to feel *peace*, to feel *potential* and to feel *power* before stepping into a situation or set of circumstances.

For example: I love repeating affirmations in my mind, writing on paper or even speaking out loud in the shower to mentally prepare for a big event.

That big event for you could be a date, and you're feeling nervous to meet someone new.

Or, let's say you get to have an annual review with your boss, and you're working up the courage to ask for the raise that you believe you deserve.

Perhaps you just want to feel in a place of peace before breaching a difficult conversation with a friend.

These are examples of when you can use the power of affirmations to affirm how you wish to first *feel* and second *create* in these situations.

Using the date situation as an example: You may be nervous because it's a first date. Rather than rest in feelings of nervousness, you can shift out of that emotion by writing or thinking the following affirmations to put yourself in a place of confidence, charisma and ease. The same can be said when asking for that raise or breaching an uncomfortable conversation.

Affirmations to Feel Good Before Your Date

- I am having a great time with my date.
- I am laughing at the things my date says.
- I am smiling at my date.
- My date is smiling at me.
- I am feeling good with my date.
- I am enjoying myself with my date.

- I am interesting to my date.
- My date is interesting to me.
- My date and I are laughing together.
- My date and I feel comfortable together.
- My heart is comfortable and beating in peace with my date.
- My mind is focused on my date.
- I am having easy conversation with my date.
- My date and I have plenty of things to talk about.
- My date is interested in seeing me again and tells me this.
- I reply that I am interested in seeing my date again as well.

Let's try the same with that raise and initiating a difficult conversation.

Affirmations to Feel Confident Before You Ask for a Raise

- I am confident.
- I am deserving.
- I am ready to receive.
- I am ready to ask.
- I am asking because my boss believes I deserve my raise.
- I am asking because my boss honors that I have the right to ask.
- I am asking because my boss will respond positively to my request.
- I am asking because my boss believes in the quality of

my work.

- I am asking because my boss believes I have great potential in this company.
- I am asking because my boss believes I should ask for what I wish to receive.
- I am asking because my boss will be pleasantly surprised that I asked.
- I am asking because it will impress my boss that I asked for what I deserve.
- I am asking because I deserve to receive this raise.
- I am asking because I get to speak to my boss with confidence.

Affirmations to Feel Secure Before Breaching a Difficult Conversation

- I am at peace with myself.
- I am at peace with this person.
- I am ready to receive the most peaceful solution from this conversation.
- I am open to hearing everything this person has to say.
- I am open to empathizing with this person about their position.
- I am open to understanding how they feel and using this as a way to find a solution.
- They are open to understanding how I feel and using this as a way to find a solution.
- They are open to empathizing with me on my position.
- We are having a safe, comfortable and open

conversation.

- We are having a conversation of positive points which empower our solution and make us feel good about ourselves.
- I am open to learning about how to be a better person from this conversation.
- I am open to letting go of my defensiveness in this conversation.
- They are open to learning about how to be a better person from this conversation.
- They are open to letting go of their defensiveness in this conversation.

Going on a first date, asking for a raise or initiating a difficult conversation are examples of situations which can build up negative energy a la nervousness, anxiety and stress if we allow uncertainty and questioning to linger in our minds.

These are events which we can anticipate for days or even weeks and when stuck in our ego-driven, fear-based minds, we default to focusing on the potential bad which could emerge!

So affirmation writing is a practice of focusing on the good before a big event in your life takes place, or the simple truth that you can always manifest your reality from a place of positive feelings and positive vibes to create positive results.

You have the power, and affirmations are the easiest and most accessible tool to access that power within no matter where you are or what you are experiencing.

Nothing is Unrealistic If You Want It

Remember how I told you about God's whisper to the heart being your voice of inspiration?

If you want it, remember that inspiration is a message of marching orders from a higher power. So if you can resonate with this belief - that you are a reflection of a higher power (God, the universe, the stars, cosmos and seven wonders of the world... *whatever!*), and that you are a reflection of this higher power in your greatness, then whatever you want is therefore *not* impossible.

In fact, your inspiration are divine orders which must be carried out to contribute to the beauty and prosperity of the world.

Some days I too doubt my greatest desires. They include traveling the world. Being a TV show host and thanks to my work in entertainment, famous. Truly meeting the *love* of my life who, without a doubt, is my soul mate and life partner.

I doubt these things simply because I have yet to experience these things.

But if these things have been proven possible for others, then why wouldn't we be able to manifest the same results for ourselves? Why them, and not us? And even most importantly: *Why not all of us?*

When we remember that what we want has already been created

in the lives of people presently living or who have come before us, we can remember that *yes!* our desires are possible. They are possible because they have *already been proven as possible by others.*

Whatever it is you wish to create rests in your heart for a reason. Trust that it's there for a purpose even if you can't wrap your head around the why or the how or the who.

You don't have to know that now, because the law of attraction is on your side, and persistence paves the path.

Exercise #3: Visualize Your Declarations

Imagine that you are an infinite source of positive, beautiful, radiating light that's beaming into the depths of the universe.

This beam of light carries the energy of your desires, your dreams and your vision in the world to attract the energy it needs to create. Whatever your beam of light is emanating becomes an image the universe sees and can 100 percent create as a physical reality on your behalf.

Visualizing your greatest desires *as real* and *already happening now* is the perfect manifestation technique to bring you into the vibrational energy of feeling good and anticipating what it is you wish to desire.

As I speak what I wish into existence, I do the following things to help give me that boost of energy which aligns my desires with what it is I'm looking to attract.

1. I Smile While Thinking & Asking for It

As you think about what it is you wish to attract, *smile!* I am smiling as I write these words, thinking about you reading this book right now and learning how to change your thoughts to change your life! Your inner well-being will magnetize your desires toward you faster and more effortlessly. Stay in a place of feeling good and when you find yourself not doing so, *just smile!*

2. I See It Appear in My Mind

When I wish for something to manifest, I allow myself to visualize it. The act of consciously visualizing will naturally illustrate the little details in my mind that I never knew I even wanted. *'Oh, you want the love of your life to have long dark hair and be at least six feet tall?'* The details which naturally present themselves on the screen of your mind is what your subconsciousness is truly desiring. Listen to the instincts revealed by your visualization!

3. I Breathe Deep & Relax About When I'll Receive It

When thinking positively, visualizing positively, speaking positively or writing positively about what I want to attract, I am in a place of peace. I breathe deep and relax. There is no rush. There is no pressure. Whatever it is I wish to have is on it's way. All I need to do is trust, love and let it go.

4. I Express Gratitude for Already Having It

What I want is already here. The love of my life is here on this planet, waiting to meet me. The financial abundance of my bank account is flowing its way toward me right at this very moment. The happiness I want is within me and I can tap into that prosperity consciousness right now without waiting around "for the future." I thank the law of attraction for being on my side by thinking or saying out loud: *'Thank you universe for all that you have given me and are giving me! Thank you for sending my desires my way. I feel them and they are here and I cannot wait to celebrate and express even more gratitude when I receive them.'* And so it is!

5. I Let Go of Attachment That It Defines My Happiness

The law of attraction works for those who are in a state of well being *right now*. Even if times are tough, there is so much for you to be grateful about. We dive deeper into the art of gratitude in Secret #6!

So if you're attached to the idea that this *one* thing will make you happy, whole and complete, then you've "future-forecasted" happiness and feel less than, not good enough or unfulfilled *right now.*

Which isn't the point. The point is that you are happy, whole and complete *now* and in this state of well-being open to receiving your highest and best as it aligns with your desires and dreams. You are happy *now because you know what you need and want is on its way.*

Secret #5

Take Awesome *Action*

*"If you go to work on your goals, your goals will go to work on you.
If you go to work on your plan, your plan will go to work on you.
Whatever good things we build end up building us."*
— Jim Rohn

AFFIRMATION
Today I can just DO it.

SONG
"Bust a Move" — Young JC

DEFINITION
Action (noun): An act that one consciously wills and that may be characterized by physical or mental activity; something done or performed; act; deed; effect or influence.

IN THIS CHAPTER, WE WILL REVIEW:

1. When I Learned to Bust a Move
2. Positively Planning your Plan
3. Creating Your Conscious Creation Plan
4. Why There is No Such Thing as No
5. Keep Swinging!
6. Evaluating Your Positive State of Mind

Busting My Moves

A few years ago I was in a friend's apartment when the book *Think and Grow Rich* caught my attention on her book shelf.

'Have you read this?' I asked her.

'No,' she replied. *'You can totally have it if you want it.'*

I took that book home and ate it up. *Think and Grow Rich* is a classic in the canon of personal success stories, written by a man named Napoleon Hill in the 1930s in response to the economically debilitating stock market crash of the '20s.

That book changed my life, especially with this simple line: *"Plan your work and work your plan."*

That statement made me realize that in order to be a success at anything, we must simply plan our steps toward that success.

Once we plan, we have a guidemap in front of us which makes what it is we've set out to do more manageable, more digestible and overall, more appealing to enthusiastically tackle and complete.

Once we have a plan, we don't feel so overwhelmed.
Once we have a plan, we feel confident we know what to do.
Once we have a plan, we have a course to follow and if needed, to pivot from.

And so with a gust of energy that could have propelled a plane across the Atlantic, I began to *"Plan my work and work my plan."*

This approach to living my life and pursuing my passions has kept me in a positive place, which considering you're reading Secret #5, you by now know is *the place you want to be!*

Because when we plan our work, we immediately step into a place of power. And to feel powerful is to feel confident. And to feel confident is to feel secure that what we do *will* have positive results and those results *will* be aligned with the intentions we've set for the manifestation we trust is on its way.

To Be a Positive Manifester is to Be a Positive Planner

"If you don't know where you are going, you'll end up someplace else."
— Yogi Berra

This is why to be a true manifester we must be a true planner.

We cannot sit around and simply meditate on what we positively believe will happen for us.

We must also take *action.*

We must believe so much in ourselves that we take action which aligns with what it is we're set on attracting into our lives.

We cannot fully vibrate with the energies behind the law of attraction until the law of attraction has your actions to *send its energy toward and stick onto.*

Remember the definition of energy: *"Derived from the utilization of physical or chemical resources, especially to provide light and heat or to work machines."*

Energy needs you *to work* in order for it have s*omething to work with*. Get it?

Without you setting yourself up to receive the energy to fuel the fire you're already lighting, there will be no where for the energy to go.

In other words: Without a plan, your energy won't be able to *stick to anything*.

Plan Your Plan & Work Your Plan

Many of us understand how to create a plan when it comes to small projects.

But when it comes to the loftier, bigger, more ambitious projects, our planning falls short. This is because the plan is never just for one hour, or one day, or even one month.

Short term planning is part of positively planning to attract the energy we wish, but using the law of attraction combined with conscious planning is more about *long term planning*. This is because long term planning asks you to address and prepare for the various steps which you may need to take to attract what it is you want.

Let's flash back to your college days, when you wrote papers with outlines to plan your paragraphs and pages.

Your *"desire outline"* would plan your future as if it were already happening - just like your outline planned your English thesis, as if it were already written.

Think of your desire outline as another vision board making activity except this particular rendition will help you to not only lay out your ideas, but brainstorm them in the first place.

You may not be a business owner, a corporation or someone who is looking to create a venture to make profits in your life, but you get to, like any business would, turn to the drawing board to outline and plan execution of your ideas.

And after outlining your ideas, you can begin to see how these are the pieces to the puzzle behind putting your plan into action, and what those little actions - which all connect to one another - will ultimately create in the grand scheme of things.

I'm going to spell out examples of "plans" with specific actions to attract two important aspects of every person's life, including yours: Love and financial freedom.

Below I've outlined example plans for taking action to align your energy with the law of attraction.

These plans may inspire you but may not be *your* best-feeling plans. And that's totally OK. Do what feels right for you by following *your* plan, sticking to *your* plan, and letting *your* plan work energy into your life, effortlessly.

The key is to do what feels best for you, because your energy will keep you focused and moving forward positively.

Desire Outline Plan #1 — Attracting the Love of Your Life

Step 1: Using a book like the *Soul Companion Exercise* (find it on Amazon), write out a list of qualities which you *want* and *do not want* in your life partner.

Begin to marinate in who this person is and how they make you feel. Imagine how you may meet, imagine the first words spoken to one another, imagine the moment you just *know* there's something special about them. Refer back to Secret #4 for inspiration on the power of visualization.

Step 2: Treat yourself like the love of your life to attract the love of your life. This means taking care of yourself via sleep, eating right, pampering yourself and wearing clothing that makes you look and feel great.

Been meaning to go on those morning runs? Start now. Been wanting declutter your apartment to create some fresh air, space and energy? Do it. Been thinking about lighting candles and having a glass of wine with every dinner which you lovingly prepare for yourself at home? Yes, because you deserve it!

If you aren't treating yourself with the dignity and respect that you wish to receive from another, how will you ever know when someone else *isn't* treating you this way? Without having experienced it for yourself, you'll have a tough time attracting that which you desire into your life since you don't even know how to *feel* that energy yourself. And as you know by now, you must feel the energy to create the physical manifestation of it.

Step 3: Put yourself in a position to meet new people, have fun, and enjoy new experiences. This could be online dating. This could be saying an enthusiastic *'yes!'* to every party invitation which hits your inbox. Or, it could be signing up for a new class, joining a club or just planning a social activity with friends every weekend. Whatever it is that will introduce you to new people, *do it!* Even if that means asking people to set you up: The universe doesn't care *how*, it just cares that *you do*.

Step 4: Accept all dates. Not every date is going to be magical, but if you're in the practice of going on dates, you're in the head and heart space to be fully present for love. You begin to *feel* love when you put yourself *out there* for love, and as you radiate this loving energy your potential for chance romantic encounters grows. I call it *"sending out the love juju,"* and it becomes your magnet for attraction wherever you go and choose to turn it on.

Step 5: After a few dates, edit your *Soul Companion* list. What have you learned from your dating experiences? What did you *love*? What did you *not* love? Edit that list so it's more appropriate to where you're at now. This is how you begin to really narrow in on who it is you wish to attract into your life. Editing your list will keep the positive energy flowing, because you are grateful for the experiences which have unfolded for you thus far to inspire your specifics for calling in *"the one."*

Desire Outline Plan #2 — Paying Off Debt & Attracting Financial Freedom

Step 1: Analyze your debt. How much do you owe? How much interest are you paying each month? Write these exact numbers down, ideally in a spreadsheet so that you can refer back and alter them as you begin to successfully pay down your debt. Each time you make an edit, it'll feel like an instant wave of gratification. This will create a habit loop, thus ensuring you want to stick to your plan.

Step 2: Review your receipts, credit card bills and cash removed from your account for the past month. If you can't remember, keep record for 30 days beginning today. Write down everything you spend money on to see where your money is going, how much you're spending and why you're spending it in the first place.

Use a spreadsheet to keep track, or simply a notebook you keep by your side at all times. You'll be amazed at where your money goes (I tend to thoughtlessly buy gum, coffee and power bars) and with a little self-control, you could be saving mega bucks to pay down your debt and step into abundance.

Step 3: After evaluating your spending habits for 30 days, decide where you can cut back. This is probably the hardest step of all, because you will have to honestly check yourself and let go thinking that you're "denying yourself" just because you stop, say, getting your nails done. Cutting back to save is not scarcity.

We must shift our thinking to the statement that, *"I don't save because I'm poor - I save because I'm rich,"* so that splurges become less frequent and smart decisions become activities you enjoy because you feel most abundant doing them.

Step 4: Write checks to yourself and use them to create financial freedom vision boards. Write the exact amount you wish to create on the check, address it to yourself, date it with a "goal" date of receipt and in the memo write why you received it.

Slip these manifestation checks in your wallet where you can find them. Put them on your fridge. Place them on the corner of your desk or use them as a bookmark for a book you're currently reading. Refer back to them, smile at them and feel the energy from them. Be grateful for the financial abundance which is effortlessly flowing toward you with opportunities to manifest and create. You are attracting the financial freedom you wish into your life.

Step 5: Talk the talk as you walk the walk by telling everyone you meet your plans to pay off your debt and attract financial freedom. This is what helped me to attract $8,000 into my life to pay off nearly the exact amount of credit card debt I was holding on to.

I told everyone I was attracting greater financial freedom into my life to intentionally pay off debt and then *bam!* A few months later I get an e-mail in my inbox which says, *"Here's a job opportunity for $8K - want it?"*

Expect the unexpected because you are speaking it into existence.

Step 6: Plan your work and work your plan.

Exercise #1: Plan Your Own Work & Work Your Own Plan

What is one thing you want to start taking affirmative steps toward completing?

It could be getting a new job, it could be attracting more money, it could be finally losing those 20 pounds you just can't seem to shake.

Brainstorm the various steps which you could partake in to jumpstart your dream. What are all the little, big, easy, hard, imaginable and unimaginable steps you could take?

It's time to plan!

STEP 1: On the first line in the space allotted below, write your goal in big bold letters. Use capital letters. Thicken the letters so that they're *extra* bold. If inspired to, add illustrations! Make it stand out so that each time you open the page, there is your goal smiling back at you.

STEP 2: Write any and all steps you may need to complete your goal so that you can see the various angles of action. Write the small steps and the big steps. Even write the steps which may impossible to take. It doesn't matter right now - all that matters is that you write them down.

For this part of the exercise there's no need to write your steps in logical order. Just write them.

YOUR GOAL:

THE STEPS:

_____
_____
_____
_____
_____
_____
_____
_____
_____
_____
_____
_____
_____
_____
_____
_____
_____
_____

STEP 3: Now you get to order the steps, and omit what may not be necessary.

Look at your list of steps and find which step makes sense first. Mark it with #1. Then find which steps makes sense next. Mark that with #2. And keep moving up and down your list determining the most logical order of an action plan using these steps to create order and organization.

If some steps seem to similar in order, batch them together and mark them with the same number, i.e. three steps marked at #10 on the list.

STEP 4: Now, using the space allotted below, write your steps in order now that you've numbered them appropriately. You may have five steps. You may have 10 steps. Heck, you may even have 50 steps!

The more steps the better, because you've identified the smaller - and more manageable - details you get to work on now to reach and attract what else you may need to 100 percent complete your goal.

Some of your steps are going to seem impossible. Have no fear! These are the steps which will be aided thanks to the law of attraction.

As you take steps up the ladder of your action plan, doing what you can with what you have now, you'll meet the people and be serendipitously placed in the circumstances you need to tackle those steps which seem impossible on your list ... *for now.*

When you've identified a step which feels impossible - such as meeting an investor or healing chronic pain - that's where you set your intentions to use the power of positive energy and attraction to work on your behalf.

You will meet that right investor ... because you are expecting the unexpected.

Your chronic pain can and will disappear ... because you believe in the manifestation of miracles each and everyday in the lives of everyone on this planet.

When you feel you've hit a roadblock, so long as you're setting the intention to believe that the impossible *is* possible, you will be presented with whatever it is you're wanting to attract on your action plan next.

REWRITE YOUR STEPS IN THEIR NEW ORDER:

_____

_____

_____

* * *

Your Hard Work is Your Fun Work

The reason we refuse to tackle the steps to our plans is because we create blocks within (i.e. those powerful thoughts of ours) which tell us we *'can't do that now,'* or *'we don't have what it takes to do that now,'* or *'we're not ready to do that now'* because so many other things are going on in our lives and we're just *so busy!*

Work is work. Right? But it is when we continue to step toward the great work - the work which we instinctively know is most important to complete - that we witness results which provide further impetus for us to carry on the path in pursuit of what it is we are attracting into creation this lifetime.

So, back to those love and abundance manifestation plans outlined earlier. Perhaps the hard work in attracting love that lasts is simply going on a date. You may be shy, or just hate meeting new people because you can't control the situation.

You look at dating as a drain on your energy. Basically, you're pessimistic because you haven't had great success so far, and so you figure, how is it going to change? Dating is just frustrating!!

Simply writing that paragraph brought me down. Because the bearer of these thoughts is placing themselves in a negative headspace by declaring that the frustrations of the past will become the frustrations of the future. Therefore, taking steps to do this hard work feels impossible because your mind is deciding that the work is hard.

But what if the work was fun? What if you changed your

perspective and decided that going on dates allowed you the opportunity to experience new places, experience new things, learn from the person before you, wear stylish clothes and have something to do every weekend?

Sounds like a pretty fun experience to me, this dating thing! See how much more energy-lifting reading that feels?

It's amazing how, as first quoted in Secret #1, *"When you simply change the way you look at things … the things you look at change."* — Wayne Dyer

Keep Asking — No Matter How Many Nos

The power of simply asking for what it is you want will radiate the positive energy that you believe in yourself enough *to* ask.

Because you are a light beam of energy, whatever you are asking for will eventually hear your call and come back to you attached to your light, like a boomerang of energy that's been thrown out and comes back, transformed and ready for you to use.

The key is to keep asking, even if the energy which returns doesn't exactly fulfill what you're wishing to create.

A few years ago I was manifesting a reality TV show. It was 2010 and I had partnered with two friends to produce a 3-minute sizzle for a show concept called Road Hug (mentioned in Secret #4) that took us nearly 6 months to plan, produce, edit and create. We built a site, a social media presence and flew to

Athens, Georgia where we filmed the sizzle.

We completed an amazing goal, but we didn't end up doing much with what we had accomplished. We had worked together and created together but because of personal projects stalling further action to fulfill our vision, we didn't stick together.

But the energy for my TV dreams remained - and the universe knew this.

Which is why a year later, I was cast for a reality TV show. Also at that time, one of my partners for the sizzle appeared on another reality TV show as a frequently appearing character. On top of that, I had developed a successful YouTube channel on vintage fashion and thrift store style which was pulling in thousands of views per video.

While Road Hug hadn't manifested to full completion (we wanted to sell and produce the concept), our energy was still drawing us to the TV world. We had beamed out the energy and so long as we still believed in ourselves, it was coming back to grab us.

Flash forward to 2014: Today, I'm working with a production company to produce and pitch another TV show. I'm a producer and host for the show. Once it's sold, I'll be back in the TV world and this time, I know in my heart, for good.

Trust that what you want is on its way because you have asked for it, taken action for it and stood by it. Don't give up on believing in your dreams, because you get to trust that when it happens for you, it happens right on time for you.

The key is to keep standing. Keep standing strong, and that strength will prepare you for your moment to shine because you'll be ready to receive, live and be rewarded by it.

Persistence Sets You Up for Success

"Failed plans should not be interpreted as a failed vision. Visions don't change, they are only refined. Plans rarely stay the same, and are scrapped or adjusted as needed. Be stubborn about the vision, but flexible with your plan." — John C. Maxwell

There is no such thing as overnight success.

What appears to happen overnight - when we wake up and find that our debt has been erased with a single job offer, or that we effortlessly met the love of our lives standing in line at the grocery store, or that we received the phone call of phone calls saying we had been nominated for the award of a lifetime - well, all these things happen instantaneously because we've been building on them via patiently and positively walking on our persistent paths.

At times it may seem we are witness to overnight success, be it the success of family, friends or celebrities who merely pop on the scene and are instantly rewarded with fame, fortune and fans.

But behind the scenes lies years of hard work preparing the receiver for that one moment of overnight success. And while anyone who is in their prime is still learning while shining (or else, they are slowly slipping away), it's true that according to the theory of Malcolm Gladwell, 10,000 hours of mastery is needed to truly own a craft and call it your own.

While your plan of action may not need 10,000 hours of mastery, this analogy can help anyone who thinks what they want to happen now should *actually* happen now.

Let go of believing it must happen now so that you keep the faith that you are sticking to your plan, learning from your plan and moving forward with your plan. Because your hard work is your fun work, and persistence paves your path.

Persistence will pave your path because by continuing to invest in your 10,000 hours (or whatever that amount turns out to be), you will see how your path's pre-conceived direction will change as you continue to walk it.

Because you will learn along the path and that learning will better show you the way.

Take the path of love attraction: Simply by being persistent and staying in the dating game, you learn what you do *and* do not like. This gives you a better understanding of all you wish to attract, and perhaps a few things you'll gladly say no to, because experience has shown that won't work for your best interests.

To know what to *say no to* is just as important as knowing what you want to *say yes to* because it gives you a pace on the path that continually gets better and better.

In other words: The persistent path is rocky at first because you're still putting in time to figure out *how* to walk it in the first place.

But with time, that persistence will pave a path which is smoother for you. And when you see the rocks and cracks you used to stumble over before, you know how and when to step over them. Because you've grown, learned and stayed persistent on the path.

Obstacles Are Opportunities

"When we tackle obstacles, we find hidden reserves of courage and resilience we did not know we had. And it is only when we are faced with failure do we realize that these resources were always there within us. We only need to find them and move on with our lives." — A. P. J. Abdul Kalam

When we have hard times, when we have confusing times, when we have times where everything feels like it's working against us, it's our choice to decide how we feel about it and to take responsibility for learning the lessons these obstacles are gifting us.

Yes. These obstacles are literally *giving us gifts* of life lessons and greater understanding of what it takes to *get done* what it is we *want done.*

When we begin to see everything which happens to us as a lesson, we stay in the universal orb of positive energy that keeps us moving forward carrying the good from what it is we just learned, versus feeling burdened and weighed down by the bad.

Again, may I reinforce: It's your choice whether you want to feel bad or feel good about a lesson in your life.

Because in the words of Louise L. Hay, *"You are the only person who thinks in your mind! You are the power and authority in your world."*

There will be times when tragedy hits. There will be times when you have a sorrow-filled story to tell. There will be times when the impossible really does seem impossible because metaphorically speaking you've had so many doors slammed in your face.

But we must not back down. We must not give up. And most importantly, we must never think we are failing only because times are tough.

Because our obstacles are presented to us so that we can become *stronger*, so that we become *smarter*, so that we can be of higher service to ourselves and others with greater understanding of *who to be* and *what to do*.

But this - like positive energy - is a choice.

Will you choose to be a victim, or will you choose to be a victor of your circumstances?

Keep Swinging

In 1923, Babe Ruth set two records: The number of strikeouts, *and* the number of home runs.

Both were records for the year. And his home run record? That wasn't broken until 1961, nearly 40 years later.

'Huh?' You may be thinking. So he *struck out the most* in a season and *hit the most home runs* in a season all in the same year?

Yes. Because he wasn't afraid to strike out when he stepped up to the plate with the intention to hit a home run. And because he wasn't afraid to strike out, he truly stepped up to the plate. And because he wasn't afraid to swing at 100 percent, he was able to hit those home runs at 100 percent, too.

Which is why you must keep swinging. And I'm not talking swinging just a little bit. I'm talking swinging *full on* into the ball so that the ball soars across the field and over the fence.

"Ahh! Ahh!" Can you hear the crowd cheering for you now?

You must also keep swinging because you must know that when you stepped up to the plate and struck out, *that at least you gave it all you got.*

At least you have no regrets. At least you have no self criticism that you could have done better. No. You did the best you could and you gave it all you got.

Rocky is famous for saying, *"Every champion was once a contender who refused to give up."*

So remember that when you strike out: Every champion was once just a contender. Remember that every contender has the same opportunity to become the champion.

You may be a contender today, but tomorrow, you can be a champion.

With planning. With persistence. With patience. With lessons learned. With striking out. And with ... *succeeding*.

Exercise #2: How Positive Are You?

Here's a brief exercise to see how you look at the glass which represents your life. It will help you to understand where your attitude may need to shift toward positive energy and away from the negative.

The point of this exercise is not to point out your weaknesses, but to empower your perspective for greater self-love, compassion for others and joy for living.

Because to be happy about your life is to be happy about that of others', as many of these questions will begin to show you.

Circle either *yes* or *no* to the 20 questions below to see how your attitude aligns with either the positive realm or the negative realm.

What is your immediate reaction? Trust that gut answer.

Most of the time, do you ...

1. Think to yourself, *'Why did this happen to me?'*
   Yes | No

2. Wonder why everyone else has the lucky breaks?
   Yes | No

3. Compare yourself to others?
   Yes | No

4. Worry about the future?
   Yes | No

5. Have frustration over the past?
   Yes | No

6. Hesitate asking for what you want?
   Yes | No

7. Analyze every decision?
   Yes | No

8. Worry about what other people think of you?
   Yes | No

9. Stop before you start?
   Yes | No

10. Criticize yourself … incessantly?
    Yes | No

11. Find it hard to celebrate other people's successes?
    Yes | No

12. Celebrate other people's successes but secretly wish you were the one reaping the benefits?
    Yes | No

13. Tell yourself you'll never have whatever it is that you
    secretly desire and want?
    Yes | No

14. Tell yourself to surrender to the fact that this (insert
    desire here) will never happen, and it's easier just to
    let it go?
    Yes | No

15. Refuse to take the advice of others because it makes
    you feel insecure?
    Yes | No

16. Stay in situations that you don't really like, but feel is
    the best you're ever going to have?
    Yes | No

17. Believe that people are out to hurt you or make your
    life harder because of the things they say or do?
    Yes | No

18. Feel frustrated or like there's a rush of anxiety-filled
    adrenaline into your body daily?
    Yes | No

19. Say you hate things, people, places, experiences?
    Yes | No

20. Feel blocked, feel like there's no way out, feel
    powerless?
    Yes | No

Count the number of "yes's" and "no's" you have. Do you swing more positive or do you swing more negative?

Note that these 20 questions dive deep into your confidence and how often you use language or words implying negativity.

If you aren't happy for others, you're feeling insecure.
If you hate something, you're choosing to see the negative.
If you play victim and blame the world, you're just getting in your own way to overcoming whatever it is that's in your way.

Take a few moments to reflect on your answers and where you may be choosing to feel or see negative. Use this information as inspiration to shift away from that mindset and toward one of celebration, gratefulness, optimism and inner strength.

Secret #6

Practice Radical *Gratitude*

"Be thankful for what you have; you'll end up having more. If you concentrate on what you don't have, you will never, ever have enough."
— Oprah Winfrey

AFFIRMATION
I am grateful for what I can give.

SONG
"Golden" — Jill Scott

DEFINITION
Gratitude (noun): Feeling or showing an appreciation of kindness; thankful; appreciative of benefits received; thankful; affording pleasure or comfort, agreeable.

IN THIS CHAPTER, WE WILL REVIEW:

1. One Man's Trash is Another Woman's Treasure
2. Why Gratitude is Your Attitude
3. How to Practice Gratitude Regularly
4. Celebrating All of Your Life All of the Time
5. The Lessons and Blessings of Hard Times
6. Why Gratitude "Attract" More Good Things
7. Love: Your Highest Vibration of Gratitude

That Terrific Trashcan

A few years ago I took a road trip with friends from New York City to Columbus, Maryland to check out the Virgin Mobile Freefest.

It was an annually occurring music festival that was offered free of charge if you were lucky enough to nab tickets online, which we had.

Only being 23 years old and working assistant level jobs, we weren't rolling in abundance to invest in a top notch hotel. But being Maryland (we were coming from the Big *Expensive* Apple, after all) we happily found an affordably priced Comfort Inn located not far from the pavilion where the concert was hosted.

The hotel was fresh, modern and for a few girls exploring life outside of the city - *fun!*

Especially for me: A gratitude addict who drops appreciation like a rap artist drops beats.

No - seriously. And this story will tell you why.

The morning after checking in to the hotel, we were greeted with a gorgeous spread of food that beckoned us with calories to fuel our dance and music-filled day.

Everyone gets excited over a complimentary buffet and it's no surprise that free eggs, waffles, cereal, muffins and an unlimited supply of coffee and tea would make just about anyone smile.

Smile we did, and after happily loading our plates and guzzling enough caffeine to wake up black bears hibernating in the dead of winter, we stood up to throw away our food and any disposable paper products.

And that's when I first saw her.

Far off in the corner was the most marvelous thing I had seen all morning. It was nestled sweetly and shining bright; a silver metallic finish that gave it a modern, minimalist appeal.
It was of moderate size, but designed with efficient placement of all necessary openings to facilitate the flow of input and output.

It stood there in its glory, a modern marvel that gave me a simple smile, joy like a child and a reason to be excited at the smallest of things.

What am I speaking of? *A trashcan.*

Upon using the super-charged, Super Human-esque trashcan at the hotel five years ago, I was caught squealing and showing my friends how *'cool this trashcan was.'*

I literally geeked out over a garbage container because to me, it was unique, innovative and worth appreciating. Simply put, it made me happy!

My friends made fun of me for the rest of the day, continuously comparing the concert to the trashcan. *'Sammy, is this set by Girl Talk better than the trashcan?'*

Or *'Sammy, how does this trashcan (referencing to one on the concert grounds) compare to the trashcan at the hotel?'*

It became a hilarious inside joke that I didn't mind being sweetly made fun about, simply because I loved relishing in that childlike joy of truly living, experiencing and marveling at the magic of the moment.

While just a trashcan for some, it represented glee and gratitude for me.

I found excitement in a small thing and it gave me wings for the entire day. In fact, even as I write these words I still smile over that moment.

Gratitude is not limited to the big things in life. In fact, if you find yourself only being grateful for the big things, you're denying yourself the joys of finding gratitude in anything and everything you do.

Which is ultimately how we want to live our lives - in a place of non-stop contentment, even for that which doesn't feel good at first or may not seem being grateful for in the first place.

The Science Behind Why Practicing Gratitude Works

Expressing gratitude is a tool for staying positive and attracting positive.

Because when you focus on what you *are* appreciative of, you forget to focus on what it is you are *not* appreciative of.

It's as if your mind can only focus on so much and by choosing to focus only the good, whatever bad may be hanging around goes unnoticed and as if by magic, disappears.

Remember being in middle school and learning a new language? You not only read it, but you wrote it and you spoke it, too. Reading, writing and speaking combine as a powerful trifecta for memorization power. When used in tandem to learn, you will more efficiently store information which can be quickly retrieved.

If you're committed to speaking, reading and writing gratitude on a daily basis, you are like a student in the school of good juju. When you need to access that memory of positive energy, it'll be there for you retrieve, receive and recite. Thank you, studying!

You may still be in the midst of a tough emotional situation, but thanks to literally reprogramming the manner in which your mind hums and purrs, you're more easily able to smile through the tears and trust that tomorrow will be a better day.

Gratitude, in other words, is a tool to practice daily which gives you strength to surrender to whatever your struggle is, versus resisting it and therefore feeling worse than you need to in that moment.

Because when we try to force a change, the friction's sparks stall us from ever getting over the hump. We're so electrocuted from the resistance we've been charging ourselves up with, that we can't see to the other side of the wall. *Ouch!*

So training your mind to grab onto gratitude - versus falling into instant victimhood - will actually help you to get over the bumps in the road faster, smoother and in more divine timing so that you have a clear heart and mind to learn the lessons you're supposed to (and are blessed to) learn.

Exercise #1: Ways to Express Gratitude Regularly

Gratitude is an aspect of positive thinking that is arguably the roots which hold strong the tree.

Water your roots of gratitude by committing to these practices. After a few weeks of conscious practice, they'll become automatic for you. You'll have trained your mind!

1. Gratitude Journaling

Gratitude journaling is the most tried and trued way to shift back to feeling what's good and forgetting to notice what's bad.

Gratitude journaling - like the act of writing affirmations - retrains the mind with repetition to focus and subconsciously only see the good.

Gratitude journaling is a daily ritual recommended for the morning or evening. When journaling, you simply write notes about what you are grateful for that's big *and* small.

It not only shifts your mind to a place of feeling good, but it shifts your inner being to a place of peace and serenity for wherever you are now. Your insides literally begin to feel good (trust me on this) and your energy toward yourself, others and life events will change.

Gratitude is love in action, and love is the secret ingredient to fueling the law of attraction.

2. Speaking in the Affirmative

I catch myself *not* speaking in the affirmative.

It's easier to speak negatively than it is to speak positively. This is because we don't want to sound "too confident" for fear others will judge us as being cocky or self-centered.

Throw that belief out the window.

When someone asks me how business is doing, rather than say *'It's doing OK'* I will say, *'Everything is amazing and what I want is on its way!'* Of course there have been times I've slipped, and this is usually because the other person's energy was low, and I was afraid to "one-up it."

Tip: Please don't ever dim your light for fear it will overwhelm another person. And do not allow another person's darkness to encroach on your brightness, either.

And if people think you're crazy for speaking affirmatively, who cares! The famous line from Will Smith's 2006 film *The Pursuit of Happyness* reminds me not to care what others think and to and keep speaking in the affirmative. No matter how crazy I may sound - even, in moments, to myself.

In the film Will Smith's character says to his son:

"Don't ever let somebody tell you ... You can't do something. Not even me. All right?

You got a dream ... You gotta protect it. People can't do somethin' themselves, they wanna tell you you can't do it. If you want somethin', go get it. Period."

3. Writing Affirmations

When you are feeling bad, turn to Secret #4 and write affirmations to feel good.

Don't let the bad feelings stay with you longer than they need to, or they will feel normal and become comfortably lodged in your subconsciousness.

You get to and deserve to use the power of affirmation writing wherever you are. Need help? Secret #4 outlines how and where to use them so that no matter the circumstances, you have this back pocket tool to turn to.

4. The Grateful Mind on 24/7 Replay

When I'm walking down the street I'll shift my mind from thinking about *'What I need to do today'* to how I love the environment around me.

I'll take a deep breath, gaze lovingly around me and choose

to think, *'I love these flowers! I love this green grass! I love these tall buildings! I love the blue sky!'*
While it may sound too simple to get excited about, seeing the blessings in the mundane around you will maintain high vibration to attract the things you want. Remember the trashcan story: Anything and everything is at your disposable to be grateful about, including this very moment as you read *LOVE YOUR LIFE!*

Celebrate Everything

Remember the song "Celebrate" by Kool and the Gang? Go listen to it right now on my site (sammyd.tv/celebrate-by-kool-the-gang-video) and then come back to this chapter.

Do it. Please. Just do it for me!!

The power behind that song is unstoppable. Reason being in life, we have the choice to celebrate or we have the choice to criticize.

All seven secrets of this book are about choice, and so that is why I present the question to you again: Will you celebrate life as a gift given to you everyday, or will you criticize it as a burden which makes you a victim?

Celebrating everything big or small makes you the victor - not the victim - of your life.

Normal situations you may think to moan about, but which you can choose to celebrate:

- Celebrate when you're in a car stuck in traffic, because you can listen to some awesome jams while you wait for the light to change.
- Celebrate that you were denied that job because obviously, something better and more appropriate for you is on the horizon.
- Celebrate that you can stand up, walk around and jump around.
- Celebrate that you can smile in the mirror today.
- Celebrate that you have options, even when you feel overwhelmed.
- Celebrate that you can share your gratitude with someone to make them feel good, and in giving you receive, because you give that same gift to yourself when giving it to another.
- Celebrate that you can always learn more.
- Celebrate that you can always love more.
- Celebrate that you can always take steps toward what it is you want to achieve in your life.
- Celebrate that you can celebrate the accomplishments, lives and dreams of others.

According to scientists, we actually aren't hard-wired to express gratitude. This is because our brains are still in the survival-of-the-fittest state which says that there's never enough because we are constantly hunting and struggling for our existence.

Thankfully, the world has changed.

But to be grateful for these changes we must retrain our mind muscles so that positive energy is a default way of *living to thrive*, and that we aren't just *living to survive*.

* * *

> **TAKEAWAY TIP:** Find yourself getting negative? Choose to celebrate whatever it is you may have criticized. Literally turn the situation upside on its head and find a silver lining in the clouds. Why? Because you can't control it with criticism - but you can positively move forward to create a solution if you choose to celebrate it.

* * *

When Being Positive Doesn't Make Sense

There will be days when that natural instinct says not to celebrate. It says that you deserve to feel bad. It says that you deserve to feel ill. It says that you should be feeling like a piece of crap because things are really tough and *'Ugh! You just can't take it anymore!'*

And this is only natural. In fact, feeling down and having negative thoughts may be part of the healing process you are supposed to experience so that you have the opportunity to be even *more* grateful for what you have and are creating in this lifetime.

You don't have to feel positive when there is death. You don't have to feel positive when there is tragedy. You don't have to feel positive when violence and hate harms the world and its people.

But we can feel positive for the lessons learned. We can feel positive for our compassion toward others when these circumstances befall them. We can feel positive for the opportunity to serve and contribute to the healing of another human being. We can remember what's most real - *love* - when circumstances present us hate, violence, human suffering or war.

Some examples of shifts from negative to positive using the power of gratitude include:

- In the face of death, we can feel grateful for our lives.
- In the face of tragedy, we can feel grateful for the love we have to give the world.
- In the face of violence, we can remember that peace is our mission, our goal, our purpose here.

There is never a reason to feel like a victim as every experience - good or bad - offers a lesson that is a blessing.

But the choice to see it that way is ultimately up to us.

Why Expressing Gratitude Will Attract What You Want in Your Life

When you are in a state of constant gratitude, you are in a state of feeling good.

And when you are in a state of feeling good, as Secret #2 explains, you are in a state of attracting more good things into your life which are a reflection of whatever you are focusing your attention on.

So if you are grateful that your family is treating you so well, you will continue to attract that positive interaction from your family … because you are focusing on it.

If you are grateful for the fact that you are a strong, healthy and happy human being … you will continue to be healthy, to be strong and to be happy.

If you are grateful that every person you meet on the path of love respects and appreciates you, you will continue to attract that into your life while also having better radar for when people who aren't respecting and appreciating you *do* enter your life.

Expressing gratitude for what we have is the law of attraction at work because in expressing what we love about our lives, we feel good, we feel love, we feel abundant.

And with those feelings being sent forth into the world, you bet more of that good juju is bound to come back to you.

Feeling Grateful Allows You to See What's Positively

Entering Your Life

When we are stuck in the clouds of victim mentality, we can't see anything past our own negative thoughts.

Even if good stuff is happening to us and for us, we can't see it because our muscles haven't been trained to pick up on the good juju that is always present in our space. It's as if it doesn't exist at all, because we simply don't choose to see it.

That's why, when it rains, it pours.

And why when it shines, that sun can stay up high all day long, baby!

Staying grateful is staying in the light, which shows the way clearly to more things and experiences and abundance to be grateful for.

But when we are in the darkness of victim mentality, our world is so dark, of course we can't see what good stuff may be trying to find its way to us.

Says the law of attraction, *"It's pitch black in here, so all I can send into this space is more blackness!"* Get it?

Be grateful, and allow that shine to guide you back into the light of your own beautiful life.

Your Body & Gratitude

Expressing gratitude can literally shift the strength of your body.

Speaking from personal experiences, while running or exercising, when I repeat *"I am grateful for my body's strength, I am grateful for my body's oxygen, I am grateful for my body's movement,"* it literally adds adrenaline to my body so that it can work harder, faster and stronger.

Try it for yourself.

Next time you're in the midst of physical activity or running up a hill like I often do on the weekends in Central Park, repeat in your mind *"I am grateful for my strength," "I am grateful for my strength," "I am grateful for my strength!"*

You'll feel the shift in your mind and the adrenaline pump into your body all while your legs, body, heart and mind work together to fuel the fire in your physical, strong self!

Express that gratitude and *get it done!*

Gratitude & Ignoring Negative Energy In Your Life

Your life is not perfect. My favorite affirmation is "I've let go of the need to be perfect today."

Perfection prevents progress. Perfection prevents action. Perfection prevents you from believing you are your best self now - which you always are, because you are always learning, loving and letting what you need come your way with grace and ease.

Now, because your life is not "perfect," that means we get to accept the fact that it's not always going to be peachy-keen. There will be circumstances and energy in your space that is beyond your control.

But you do not have to give the negative attention. Rather, you can choose to bless it with the positive. Because remember the entire basis of the law of attraction: What you give your attention to grows and becomes what you continue to attract into your life.

So if there is someone who says things on social media which triggers you (trigger meaning, makes you feel upset or ill at ease), when you choose to ignore what they say you are empowering your positive energy flow.

If someone or something is making your life more difficult than you'd like, choose to give the situation love, compassion and understanding. Withhold a tongue of animosity, defensiveness and anger.

In other words, giving a tough situation or encounter your negative energy will not remove the negative energy from the situation. It will in fact make the situation worse for you because as the law of attraction preaches: What you give your attention to creates more energy behind whatever it is you are focusing on.

So if you are constantly focused on negative relations with your boss, then the negative relations with your boss continue to grow or at the very least, remain a nuisance for you.

But if you choose to give your boss your vibrational energy of love and compassion, and you choose to see them as someone just like you who wants to feel loved and to feel safe? Your energy level toward them will shift to positive and that will change their energy toward you in return.

Sounds magical. Sounds mystical. Sounds … *marvelous!* And the even more more marvelous thing is that *it works.* Because how you give energy to people is how you will receive energy back from them. Perhaps not right away, but with loving patience and persistence, their softer side will be revealed to you.

TIP: There's nothing to be ashamed about when it comes to ignoring the negative, too. This is often a question I receive: *"Shouldn't I at least notice the negative so I can do something to solve it?"*

There's nothing you can do with the negative energy others give you. All can and should do is simply give that which is negative energy your positive energy. And so if you wish to consciously do something with negative energy, you simply stand strong in the powerfully positive presence you already are and can choose to access in any given moment.

If there is a squabble or something negative which arises, you will be so in the gratitude zone that it won't even matter to you. That tongue-in-cheek comment on your Facebook status update that used to bother the heck out of you?

After a few weeks of commitment to thinking and creating positive, you may not even notice it! And because you don't notice it, you don't give attention to it, and it becomes a small spark that disappears as fast as it was ignited.

* * *

TAKEAWAY TIP: There is no frustration, fear, anxiety, conflict or other negative set of circumstances which can be solved with negative energy. All good things come from good energy. Want a solution? Give it love and allow that positive energy to reveal a better set of circumstances.

* * *

Exercise #2: 10 Things to Do on the Regular to Feel More Grateful

1. **Make one positive posting on social media everyday.** Make it your declaration to feel and create good! For inspiration, follow my social media campaign for daily motivation, Lipstick Affirmations on my Instagram account: instagram.com/sammydtv

2. Upon waking or during your lunch break, **send a few positive text messages to friends, family, co-workers.**

Express that you care and wish them an amazing day.

3. **Journal why you are grateful for life in the morning or in the evening.** Use one journal (tip: keep this journal separate from the one with your to-do lists!) and commit to 10 minutes of free-flow gratitude writing.

4. Take a few minutes to scroll through Facebook or Instagram and **literally like and celebrate everyone's post,** no matter who it is. This allows you to let go of grudges and the belief that you shouldn't interact with a particular person's post just because they may not *"appreciate it."* Who cares! Show your appreciation for what they're up to because they are an awesome human being, *just like you.* It will make you feel good and create a channel with space for positive energy to be sent back to you, too.

5. **Look at people in their eyes** at the cash register, restaurant, check out line, anywhere! Address them by their first name (if you see it on a name tag) and **smile at them.** Literally - *smile!*

6. Speaking of smile, **smile as much as possible.** If you're on a computer often, try to smile while you are on the computer. Smile for no reason as you walk down the street or drive your car. Smile at the trashcan in your kitchen. *Go ahead, do it! I know you want to!*

7. **Give away your unneeded things.** I find the most radical happiness from simply giving away things I no longer need to those who could benefit from them or feel good from the joy of an unsolicited gift.

8. **Say silent prayers.** You don't need to go to a church or have read religious text to pray. Prayer connects you to feelings of peace, prosperity and a sense of purpose.

Upon waking in the morning, pray to your higher power within in thanks for all that you are and are about to experience that day. When I wake up I try to make my first thought be, *'Dear day, thank you for all that I am about experience, live, love and learn. I am grateful!'*

9. **Frequently send thank you notes, emails and phone calls.** It means the world to the receiver to read just a few lines of thanks from you. It doesn't have to be a big deal. But especially when it comes to standing apart for job interviews, future relationships and business deals, a thank you note can really go a long way and make you a memorable face and not just another person someone randomly met at a networking event or mixer.

10. Wherever you are and whomever you're with, **see the person before you as someone in need of love, safety and serenity**, *just like you.* There is an inner child within us all. When we choose to see that innocent child in ourselves and those around us, we remember that there is no reason to feel separate or fearful of one another. We are connected as adults, just like we were as young children without judgement or discrimination.

How to Be Grateful for and Celebrate the Powerful, Beautiful & Special You

Love letters change your way of being so rather than *self-criticize*, you *self-celebrate*.

For most people who are healing from their own self-loathing, writing a love letter is an awkward, unnatural thing to do.

In fact, writing is an uncomfortable activity for most people in general. This is because writing is where your true soul is revealed, because you are not communicating to another person or using a piece of technology to transcribe your thoughts.

Rather, you are writing to yourself. Your eyes only. Your heart, your mind, your life. *There*. On paper.

And when pulling out that pen to write, you can either lie to yourself or be honest with yourself.

I encourage you to adopt the practice of writing love letters to you (*yes, you!*) on a daily basis for at least a week.

Writing yourself a daily love letter for seven days will help reset that self appreciation button. You'll remember the things you love about yourself that you may have forgotten or, somewhere along the way, decided weren't good enough to regularly celebrate.

Your love letters will reveal that *yes*, they are good enough to celebrate and *heck yes!* You've got a lot going on worth celebrating and being grateful about in the first place.

Need help writing your love letter? Visit my site (sammyd.tv/dear-me-i-love-you-because) for instructions on how to write the love letter for you.

Love letters celebrate the awesomeness of you *right now* - because everything about you is remarkable and worth celebrating. You could be a member of the senate or a server at the local restaurant. It doesn't matter what you do or have done because no matter your accomplishments, we are each divine creatures here to offer the world our gifts.

I've written myself dozens of love letters. I picked up the technique during a period of intense self exploration in my life. I needed to reset my self love button and writing the love letters showed me just how sensitive I was to truly expressing radical self love *to myself*.

I would literally begin to cry when the love letter hit a tender point which it inevitably would because when we write to ourselves, our true selves are revealed.

My advice for a love letter newbie: No matter how awkward it may feel at first, writing your first love letter is like doing a tough workout for the first time.

It's going to feel uncomfortable, and you won't know all the moves, and maybe afterwards you'll be sore for a few days.

Because writing yourself a love letter may just turn the water on, which is a good thing: Strong people shed strong tears, and to have this happen is a good sign that you are moving in the direction of self-love because you are embracing *all* of your emotions with greater awareness of who you truly are, more confidently letting go of limiting beliefs you may have about yourself.

You are a beautiful, powerful and special person. When you

begin to recognize this through the power of love letters, you will begin to be that person without doubts and with 100 percent self-trust of your authentic desires. You will truly live in a more peaceful, powerful presence which will maintain your vibration of feeling good.

Love Vibration Is Gratitude Vibration

Love vibration is the strongest vibration of gratitude on the planet.

Why? Think back to the last time you were in love.

And maybe you weren't really in love, but rather had an infatuation, or a little romantic fling that was bubbling its good juicy juju at the time.

You probably felt one of the following:

1. I'm high as a kite!
2. I'm on Cloud 9!
3. Everything is beautiful!
4. I'm *so* excited, I just can't hide it!
5. Dude, I'm on top of the world!

1-5 essentially mean all the same things: That you were experiencing a state of euphoria because you were calibrating on the emotion of love.

For those of you who have seen *500 Days of Summer* (starring Joseph Gordon-Levitt and Zooey Deschanel), you may remember the scene where Joseph Gordon-Levitt's character is dancing around the city after having had a date with Zooey Deschanel's character.

As he danced, he was completely oblivious to how he looked and seemed to be experiencing his own euphoric reality.

This is what we call the natural high, and at its *highest* height. Now here's the shocking reality for some of us: It's possible to *always* be in this super euphoric state, but *not* because you have a boo who is texting you romantic one-liners and their most sexy selfies.

You can feel this state of euphoric bliss because through the act of gratitude, celebrating life, seeing every encounter as a holy one and working on loving yourself, you begin to *simply love for the sake of simply loving.* You don't need someone or something else to affirm it. You are just, plain and simple, *love.*

And isn't that a powerful state of being: To love for the sake of simply loving?

The thread which weaves the law of attraction, conscious creation and positive thinking is the never-changing truth *that love is all we need.*

And so living, breathing and learning all of your life from a place of love is how we can overcome anything and everything, because love is always the higher power, and love is always leading you the best way.

Secret #7

Meditation Manifests Your Magic

"To understand the immeasurable, the mind must be extraordinarily quiet, still."
— Jiddu Krishnamurti

AFFIRMATION
I am patient because I am powerful.

SONG
"Stillness of Heart" — Lenny Kravitz

DEFINITION
Manifestation (noun): An event, action, or object that clearly shows or embodies something, especially a theory or an abstract idea; a sign that shows something clearly; one of the forms that something has when it appears or occurs.

IN THIS CHAPTER, WE WILL REVIEW:

1. A Swimmer's Story: Visualizing My Success
2. How to Make Visualization Work for You
3. Using Visualization to Believe in What You Want
4. The Benefits of Daily Meditation
5. Resources for Meditation Practice & Instruction
6. 3 Shifts for Meditative Peace
7. Trusting Your Vision

If You Can See It, You Can Be It

It's a popular statement in the self development world, an almost cliché expression which deserves a line of T-shirts, coffee mugs and a hashtag on Instagram for motivational postings.

But we must remember that clichés are clichés for a reason, because for the most part, they've been proven true.

I discovered the strength of "seeing it to be it" when I became a competitive swimmer at seven years old.

My father taught me the art of visualization. He told me to stand on the swimmer's starting block and imagine myself diving swiftly into the water.

He told me to feel the strength of my arms pushing me through the water. He told me to see how I would hit the wall and effortlessly flip, turning with elegance and grace below the water so I could quickly emerge to the surface for my second lap toward the other end of the 25 meter length pool.

He told me to see myself ahead of the other swimmers, the gap increasing with each of my powerful strokes until finally, I tapped the wall, victorious and in first place.

Stroke. Stroke. Stroke. Head in the water. No breath needed. My body's strength pushing me to the end of the pool lane.

Hit the wall. First place.

I would see myself swim the entire race beginning to end, counting the seconds I wanted it to take and the breaths I would need so that my body would be able to *respond* to the visualization when asked to *physically reproduce* it.

It's the mind-body connection that athletes and scientists to mystics and spiritual leaders will speak about. It's a connection between your body and your mind, as if your body was the plug and your mind is the cord. Once connected, you've got a channel of energy to do whatever you set your mind out to do because your body is fully connected to it.

I've used the same strategy when bowling: Before stepping out to throw my ball, I visualize and literally feel how the ball will leave my fingers and - rolling swiftly and strongly in the center of the lane - hit all 10 pins so that I can celebrate a strike.

* * *

TAKEAWAY TIP: Follow the expression *"Keep your eye on the prize"* by visualizing yourself doing, succeeding and winning. Having trouble visualizing your vision? The following exercises will help work your visualization power so that it's activated for your reality-come-powerfully-true.

* * *

Exercise #1: How to Make Visualization Work for You

1. Choose to See Yourself in Possession of What It Is You Desire

Let me ask you this: What is it you want to achieve in your life next? It can be big, it can be small, it can already be a work in progress.

Whatever it happens to be, choose to see yourself, in your mind's eye, in possession of what it is you wish to create.

Because when we see ourselves in possession of what we wish, we can begin to feel the emotions associated with actually having it. And as we've learned so thoroughly in the seven secrets behind the law of attraction, when we are calibrating in the celebratory energy of having what it is we desire, then we put out the positive energy to actually *attract it into our lives*.

My Visualization Success Story

Last fall, I stood in the kitchen of my Manhattan apartment and felt my spiritual partner by my side. A few weeks earlier, I had just told a man I had been dating that I was no longer interested in seeing him. I told him I wanted a committed relationship and didn't feel the right energy to move our relationship in that direction.

By ending that relationship and declaring what I truly wished, I had consciously created space to visualize and call in what I truly wanted next, which was my spiritual partner.

As I stood in my kitchen calibrating on this desire, I literally felt his presence on this planet and began to cry *trusting* that he was here. The tears were tears of joy because I just knew that *yes!* he would show up in my life. I had no doubts.

A few weeks later, I met him. He was a member of the same meditation school I attend, and we were instantly romantically and spiritually connected.

The only problem with our fated meeting? He ended up being, at the time, in another committed relationship.

It was like *Romeo & Juliet:* two fated lovers who, due to circumstances beyond their control, could not be together.

So what did I learn from that experience? I hadn't called in a spiritual partner who would be my life partner! While calibrating on this man I knew would have significant impact on my life, I hadn't specifically declared he would be available for a committed relationship. And so I didn't have the law of attraction to blame - I had me.

And so while he and I will always connect on the spiritual plane, in this lifetime we may never connect as committed partners walking the same path. And that's OK.

He remains my spiritual partner today, often sharing meditations, readings and sending check-in texts to see how I'm doing. In fact, I do the same for him. And so, while we've never addressed it, perhaps he called me in as his spiritual partner, too.

The power of visualization is not just a tool to call in, but to ask yourself *'What is it that I truly want?'* so that you see what it is you *truly* want, and not just what the world says you *should* want.

2. Behave as if You Already Have What It Is You Want

Want to be more loved? Behave as if you *are loved* by smiling at every single person you meet.

Want to be abundant? Express *so much radical gratitude* for all the amazing things in your life which continuously show up and and shine on you. Speak out loud how much you love this, or appreciate that, or are so excited and thrilled that this is happening to you!

Want to get a new job? Tell everyone *'you have it in the bag'* and *'know that the best opportunity for you is on its way.'* Even if that dream job doesn't manifest right away, you are speaking into existence the fact that your dream job is here now and is here *now for you!* You already have that job, it's just a matter of stepping into it when the law of attraction presents it to you.

We speak what it is we wish into existence as if its already here. All the love I want? Is here! All of the abundance I want? Is here! All the goals accomplished, plans fulfilled, big dreams made reality, *is here!*

Call in what you desire by proclaiming that it is a part of you right now. It is a reality for you right here, right now.

3. Believe You Deserve What It Is You Wish to Manifest

We cannot manifest, attract or create what it is we desire if we don't believe we deserve it first.

This is why we must also take action toward what it is we want because in taking action, making moves and following our plans, we are investing in ourselves and therefore believe in ourselves because the results of our actions have proven so.

When I called in my spiritual partner, I sincerely believed that I deserved him. I was at a place in my life where I needed spiritual guidance. I was looking for it to help me and because

I believed in helping me, I believed I deserved this person's energy.

The same could be said of believing you deserve to lose weight, or have increased financial freedom, or take a pleasurable vacation. You deserve these things because they make you a happier, healthier and more loving person.

When you are calibrating on this positive energy, you are making the world a better place. You deserve to feel good so that you can help the world feel good, too.

We tend to block attracting what it is we want because *we don't believe that we deserve it.* There is still an insecurity that once we have it, we are going to lose it or worse yet, it will be returned to its previous owner because we weren't good enough to receive it and they figured us out.

So not true!! It's that little voice of doubt which keeps us from attracting the greatness we deserve to have. Until we can decide we are great, we will only attract good. And if we're only attracting good? Work to change your beliefs about what you deserve to have.

Changing internal beliefs about what you believe you deserve to have is the same as changing your self-concept, as addressed in Secret #1.

Here's an example of how to write affirmations to affirm that yes, you deserve to meet the love of your life!

Example — Affirmations That You Deserve to Meet the Love of Your Life

- **I believe that I deserve the love of my life** because I have spent time dating and getting to know the many personalities in the world, as well as my own.

- **I believe that I deserve the love of my life** because I am ready for love and am ready for the fulfilling work love brings.

- **I believe that I deserve the love of my life** because I give love, therefore I am worthy enough to receive love.

- **I believe that I deserve the love of my life** because I believe that I am the love of my life.

How You May Be Accidentally Negatively Visualizing

It's OK to be nervous, it's OK to be a little insecure (as we're always improving), it's OK to not feel perfect in everything we do (it's about progress, not perfection, anyway).

But when we expect the worse, or look to the past as reason for what we believe will happen in the future, or see the worst in our minds and focus only on that, then we are negatively visualizing the future and attracting the negative energy - and manifestation - of whatever it is we fear happening in the first place. *Woops!*

Remember that the law of attraction works both positively and negatively: If you're sending out fear-based energy, you will attract more of the reality in alignment with whatever it is you fear.

By feeling the energy of scarcity, uncertainty and lack of confidence, you will bring more of that to the table of your life. On the table will manifest what you were hoping wouldn't happen in the first place.

But there it is, again, because you worried it into existence.

You can worry things into existence because you are focusing on the bad, and not shifting back to the good.

You have chosen a negative set of possibilities and forget that you can throw that negativity out of the window and tell yourself, see yourself, affirm yourself, be grateful about yourself with a new story of hope, love, expectation and abundance!

Positive thinking is seeing your life as a blank slate of positive creation in every moment. Allow your past to inspire change - not to create constraints.

How to Lessen the Negative Visualization

The next time you feel yourself in a state of worry, let go of the worries by smiling to yourself and saying in your mind, *'Not this, not this.'*

This is a gentle way to mentally exit from a negative situation created by your mind without criticizing yourself for going there or feeling that way in the first place.

Because again, it is only natural to have a doubt, worry, fear or insecurity from time to time. We're only human!

And that's the good news: *We're only human!* And being human, we always have a choice. We can always shift out of the negative feeling and step into a positive feeling. We can always erase the board of a negative visualization, grab some brightly colored markers and paint ourselves a more positive visualization.

We are not victims of our minds, just like we're not victims of our circumstances. Your higher self has the power to choose. You are more powerful, beautiful and special than you think.

Adopting a Daily Meditation Practice

Daily meditation has been the most transformative activity of my life.

With the regular clearing of my thought-filled mind, I am less attached to the negative voices in my head which tell me to feel bad about this or that, or which visualize the worst, or which bring me down with false ideas of loneliness, depression and not being happy enough or on the right path.

During meditation, I return to a feeling of love for the sake of love, joy for simply being alive, acceptance of what is and full trust that the best for me is always on its way because since energy is neither created nor destroyed but simply exists ... *it is already here.*

But we must quiet our minds to clear away bad energy so that our still minds can be open to receive the good energy.

If you imagine your mind is like an empty glass which fills up with water each and everyday, you will understand why you need to meditate: To empty it of the old, dingy, lukewarm water that has collected in the glass of your mind.

We don't drink dirty water, so why would you want to keep thinking dirty thoughts? (Not *those* kind of thoughts - but the negative ones).

Meditation cleanses your mind so that the love, the light and the positive thoughts can more clearly rise to the surface and remain with you throughout the day.

What is Meditation and How You Can Learn

Meditation is an ancient practice descending from India and which in original form, involved repetitive rhythmic chants to improve concentration and clarity as a spiritual practice for enlightenment, which according to Buddhism is a *"Final blessed state marked by the absence of desire or suffering."*

Meditation is a means of transforming the mind so that you develop an internal state of well-being and improve your concentration, clarity, emotional positivity and a calm perspective of the true nature of things.

There are a variety of philosophies and disciplines surrounding meditation that you can refer to either online or, if near you, attend in a school setting.

There is no one right way to meditate and often what you started as a meditation practice will evolve with time and growing understanding of what you need.

Exercise #2: Give Stillness a Try

The suggested way to meditate is to find a comfortable, private place to sit so that you can place both feet flat on the floor or sit cross-legged in the lotus position.

You can meditate anywhere, but if you are in a public space you will naturally be more uncomfortable than if you were in a private space away from the eyeballs of those you don't know.

Set your timer for 10 to 15 minutes.

Close your eyes and relax. Allow yourself to simply sit for a moment. Whatever comes up for you in your heart and your mind or felt by your body is OK. Again, there is no right way to meditate.

After a minute of sitting, begin to consciously take deep breaths inhaled through your nostrils and exhaled from your mouth. Try one right now, just for practice.

Breathe. As you exhale, imagine all tension is exiting from your body.

Continue breathing deep with a slow and steady rhythm. Find an inward focus so that you feel you're in an open space. Perhaps even visualize that you're sitting in a field.

Various meditation practices will introduce you to a mantra which you can repeat in your mind so that unnecessary thoughts capture less of your attention.

The adoption of a mantra is a very personal thing and so I will not suggest one for you here, however know that it is an option for you, especially if you enroll in a meditation school or work with a meditation teacher.

As the thoughts come and go, gently and lovingly return your mind to a sense of stillness and silence. Use the thoughts as a means to transition away from the clutter and back to the wide, open space.

Continue to breath, letting go of self criticism, or seeking of a perfect meditation goal. Just be.

When your timer goes off, sit in stillness for another minute. Listen to the sounds you hear around you. Feel the weight of your body on the chair, or the brush of air on your face. Relish in you. Smile.

Open your eyes. See the world as if new for the first time.

———————————————————————————

Resources for Meditation Practice

In episode #10 of *SAMMYD TV, I interviewed meditation instructor Ritu Ashrafi about meditation and why we should turn to it as a part of our daily routine. You can watch that episode here: tinyurl.com/sammydtv-meditation.

Ritu Ashrafi is a meditation instruction who offers an online course via her site, The Lifester. You can sign up for her free 5-day meditation video series here: http://simplymeditationonline.com/free

For the sake of introducing you to the benefits of meditation as easily as possible, here are some resources for meditation which you can refer to right now.

Some of the following apps are free, while others may cost a few dollars (totally worth it!). Look them up in your phone's app store and choose the one which works best for you.

Meditation Apps
Get Some Headspace
Mindfulness
Simply Being
Meditate
Mindfulness Meditation
Calm
Breathe2Relax
Buddhist Meditation Trainer

Omvana
Take a Break!
Relax Melodies
MINDBODY Connect
Buddhify 2

Meditation & Visualization Videos

Here's a selection of instructional videos for meditation and visualization from Positive Magazine, a YouTube channel of empowering videos for positive thinking and feeling.

Watch here: tinyurl.com/positivemagazineplaylist

1. 10-Minute Guided Meditation to Ease Anxiety, Worry and Urgency

   Watch here: tinyurl.com/guidedmeditation-1

2. 10-Minute Guided Meditation for Positive Energy

   Watch here: tinyurl.com/guidedmeditation-2

3. 10-Minute Guided Meditation for Removing Manifestation Blocks

   Watch here: tinyurl.com/guidedmeditation-3

How Meditation Will Begin to Work on Your Behalf

1. Stronger Intuition & Self-Trust

We all have a sixth sense, but we can't use it unless clear of any dirt, muck and mess surrounding it.

Imagine your sixth sense is like a knob on the dashboard of your car that you don't need to use but which will occasionally benefit you.

Like your high beams. It's not everyday you need to use them, but they really come in handy on the highway when little lights are in sight to help guide your path.

Your sixth sense - like your high beams - is the ultimate illumination. So when we clean that knob, add some oil or W-40 so it's able to move, we can more easily turn it on when we need to use it.

Meditation is the cleaning wipe, the oil, the W-40 that your sixth sense needs to stay a clean knob on that dashboard which will turn effortlessly when necessary.

We need our intuition for those tough moments when we want to turn within to reveal an inner truth. We also need our intuition to confidently guide us on the path of making and trusting our decisions.

Ever meet someone, and you think to yourself, *'My intuition tells me this person is going to be my friend?'* And of course, that manifests as true because you've affirmed it so.

That intuition can be applied to business deals, potential romantic partners, winning at games of chance, and even when deciding whether you should or should not go to an event.

Your intuition is an emotionally-charged, magnetic pull. It's an inner voice that becomes louder the more stillness you gave your space in order to hear it.

Intuition can also pull you away from a potentially negative experience. The power of intuition strengthens the sound of your gut which may say, *'This doesn't feel right,'* when a particular option is presented to you.

You can ask for guidance from your intuition with every decision. The best way to call upon the strength of your intuition is ask your heart how it feels about Option A versus Option B in regards to making a decision concerning a particular situation.

Your heart will speak to you using the power of feeling. The wrong option will feel icky, while the right one will feel much better. Or perhaps both options feel good or both options feel bad.

Either way, asking your heart is the easiest way to access your intuition, but practicing daily meditation will open your intuition to natural consciousness so that no matter what, you are trusting your gut because your gut is communicating to you loud and clear.

2. **You Become Open & Aware of Synchronicity in Your Life**

With an open mind, you have the capacity to notice signs which are naturally occurring in your life because the universe is a self-ordering being of power.

Because meditation helps to clear the mind of clutter, you're in a higher place of presence to simply notice how you are vibrationally connected to the world, because as you think of things, there they will be.

You'll feel compelled to call someone and upon answering they say, *'I was just thinking of you.'*

You'll step into a grocery store thinking of a product to purchase when *voila!* There just so happens to be a sale on it and free sampling of its new flavors available.

You'll be told to see a movie, speak to a person, or read a book numerous times and finally cave, as it keeps showing up in your life and must, therefore, mean something of significance.

You'll see things multiple times in one day, you'll notice a number on the clock everyday for a week, you'll think about someone and they'll text you later that day.

The power of meditation is unlimited, as it taps into the power you were born to be and have, but which the layers of life have buried deep inside you and which, with decluttering of negative energy which doesn't serve you, can rise slowly and strongly to the top of your consciousness.

3. Your Peace Becomes Your Power

Meditation breaks through the layers of anxiety, insecurity, confusion and any emotion which is of low vibration and low energy, as referenced in Secret #2.

The daily practice of stillness clears your mind and reveals your calm nature to see the "true nature of things."

And what is the true nature of things? Everything is OK and most of the time, we are creating a story of struggle which can be rewritten as quickly as it was written.

Meditation melts away the false belief that we need to worry in the first place, therefore allowing the power of peace to become an energy you carry with you throughout the day.

I feel a much greater sense of peace after I've meditated. It's as if I've just opened the door to a dark room, turned on the light and taken a dust cloth and broom and swept away the dust bunnies to reveal a cleaner, fresher and more sparkling room in my mind.

I feel love for myself, my life and whatever it is that I'm creating that day. I feel gratitude without even asking for it. I feel secure and safe in who I am, without a desire to push to become anything else. I know that whatever I need is on its way, and where I'm at is perfect and divine.

When I feel the power of peace, I question myself less. I take the right steps toward the right action. I learn, I live, I love.

Peace is our power to experience and truly feel the fruits of life.

4. **Your Wise Voice Within Becomes Louder**

In the midst of meditation I've heard a wise voice speak without my mind provoking or asking it.

It's as if this wise voice just pops in to say in a very Zen-like fashion, *'Here is your lesson for the day.'*

I refer to this voice as "the wise woman within." Her temporary interruptions to my meditation offer a pearl of wisdom which speaks silently, but at moments you are in complete stillness.

It was said by ancient sage Lao Tzu, *"Be still / Stillness reveals the secrets of eternity."*

If stillness presents the secrets of eternity, those secrets of eternity must be revealed to you in some shape or form in conjunction with the power of meditation.

Whether by synchronicity, intuition or a wise voice which

mysteriously speaks from within, regular meditation reveals uncanny moments of "a-ha" telling us how to peacefully and confidently step forward on our path.

How to Motivate Your Visualization & Meditation Practice

Visualization and meditation is easier said than done. I speak from personal experience!

I do my best to meditate in the morning, but life can get in the way. Which is why when I feel a resistance to meditation arise, I drop everything and tell myself to, *'just meditate.'*

It will take some practice to consciously adopt these practices into your daily routine. But like any habit, you can start now to form the habit loop and make it so you can't *not* meditate or find stillness during the course of your day.

I suggest looking to meditation as a commitment to mental health that, much like going to the gym, you carve out time for and even schedule on your calendar.

Meditation can take place wherever you make it happen, although ideally you're in a quiet, comfortable and private space. Some ideas for the busy 9-to-5er may include:

a. At home before work.
b. Standing in the shower.
c. In your car while sitting in the parking lot of your job or any other establishment you may be.

d. During your lunch break.
e. On the toilet at your office!
f. While taking public transportation.
g. In a nearby park.
h. Before you go to sleep as a way to calm the mind and prepare the body for rest.

If you begin to notice a resistance to your meditation practice, that is OK. This will naturally happen because as you meditate regularly, you will begin to more strongly experience a consistent state of feeling good. So when times are good, sometimes we let go of doing all that which helped them to be good in the first place.

Again, the analogy of working out is a beautiful one for meditation. If you stop working out, you will lose the tone, the energy, the svelte shape. And so if you stop meditating, you will feel similar effects within your out-of-shape mind.

Additionally, meditation may not feel very productive for you. You may think to yourself, *I can be doing better things with myself during this time.'*

You must decide that these techniques of stillness via meditation and visualization, while they don't feel like they're doing anything in the moment, are planting seeds of benefits which will quietly sprout and support you on your path.

What you reap is what you sow. Meditation allows you to sow good energy, good vibes, good attraction each and everyday for a garden that can last for a lifetime of beauty and bliss.

Trusting Your Desires

Meditation and visualization are tools to erase a chalkboard of negative energy so that we can more easily write our stories of positive energy which will attract everything we wish and believe we deserve into our lives.

Adding these exercises of stillness into our daily regimens are integral for staying in the space of feeling good.

When I begin to feel frustrated or ill at rest, I turn inward to take a few deep breaths and repeat my mantra to find a center of ease, enthusiasm and energy.

I know that something is off with my meditation and visualization practice when I begin to lose trust in what it is I am doing, desiring or creating at any given moment.

Meditation and visualization practices will keep you in a place of self-trust. The fears, the insecurities, the anxieties will become less prominent in your mind and if they appear, you have the sense of security to say *'Phooey! You are a bunch of BS [or insert favorite expletive here].'*

Even as I write this book, questions of its worth and validity arise in my mind.

I have the power to see those doubts but not be those doubts.

Thanks to meditation this morning, I'm more easily able to notice when I'm off focus from my writing and, because I've learned the value of compassion toward everyone - especially myself - lovingly guide myself back to the task at hand.

Regular meditation and visualization will continue to reaffirm what it is you really want so that you know what to say no to and what, with this awesome abundance and positive energy which is bubbling within, you wish to passionately pursue, create and manifest into your life.

In Conclusion — Trusting Yourself

To know yourself is to trust yourself. You know yourself so well in areas of your life that there's no question when making a decision.

An example may be your favorite foods, or favorite color, or even favorite sleeping position. If someone asks you any of the above, you confidently answer. There is no hesitation or feeling of insecurity with your answer.

But is this the truth in all areas of your life? Do you confidently answer what you want in a life partner, a dream job, a hobby, a life worth living?

These answers will ebb and flow, but they can and deserve to change with confidence. Meditation and visualization offer you that confidence of trusting *your* character. It is not trust which is cocky or condescending, but which simply knows.

The more we find stillness and erase that chalkboard of cluttered thoughts, the more *who we truly are* and *what we truly want* is revealed to us.

The late Osho, who served as an Indian mystic, guru and spiritual leader for his lifetime until his death in 1990, explains knowing thyself with this quote well.

> *"Nobody can say anything about you. Whatsoever people say is about themselves. But you become very shaky, because you are still clinging to a false center. That false center depends on others, so you are always looking to what people are saying about you. And you are always following other people, you are always trying to satisfy them. You are always trying to be respectable, you are always trying to decorate your ego. This is suicidal. Rather than being disturbed by what others say, you should start looking inside yourself. Whenever you are self-conscious you are simply showing that you are not conscious of the self at all. You don't know who you are. If you had known, then there would have been no problem — then you are not seeking opinions. Then you are not worried what others say about you — it is irrelevant! When you are self-conscious you are in*

*trouble. When you are self-conscious you
are really showing symptoms that you
don't know who you are. Your very self-
consciousness indicates that you have not
come home yet."* — Osho

To know thyself is a lifelong journey because yes, life produces circumstances which produce change and yes, the only thing constant in life is change to begin with!

But through the power of stillness we can return to the essence of who we are - love, peace, compassion, infinite wisdom and opportunity - and as we walk forward on our unique life paths, know ourselves every step of the way.

When there is a fork in the road, we know which way to take.

When there is a bump in the road, we know how best to navigate it, for us.

When there is a need to pause and rest on the road, we do so.

When there is a need to speed up and sprint on the road, we make this happen because we believe in us.

To love your life is to love yourself in this moment now, trusting you have everything you need.

The exercises, anecdotes and tips of this book are merely to show that *you already have the power.*

Like Dorothy discovers in *The Wizard of Oz*, the power you've been searching for has been inside you all along.

Dorothy walked the yellow brick road thinking she would be happy once she reached her destination to meet the Wizard. She believed he had the power to help return her home to happiness again. She was so focused on the destination that she didn't realize how the entire time on the yellow brick road - metaphorically representing the journey of life - she actually had the power to return home the entire time!

Which is why the movie ends with her ruby slippers activating the power she wanted in order to return home to Kansas. Dorothy was looking to external sources to make her dreams a reality when in truth, she had the power within her all along. In fact … *she was wearing it!*

You are more powerful, beautiful and special than you think. There is a divine reason you are on this planet, and there is an even more divine reason you purchased *LOVE YOUR LIFE!* to read and learn the power of positive thinking and attraction which rests inside of you *right now.*

Welcome to a life you love - no wizard granting your wishes for happiness necessary.

Rather, *you are the wizard.*

Because you are more powerful, beautiful and special than you think.

YOUR FINAL THOUGHTS

Congratulations!!!

You have successfully completed *LOVE YOUR LIFE! The 7 Secrets to Using the Power of Positive Thinking & Law of Attraction to Create the Dream Life for You!*

I am so, so thrilled for you. You just took a trip and it was called learning about yourself, how you feel and what you *truly* wish to feel so that you can attract what it is you *truly* want … for the life you *truly* wish!

You may have thoughts left to share. Writing them here will maintain the energy of this workbook. Take a few minutes to share with yourself how you are feeling in this very moment. Take a stream of consciousness approach and write whatever it is that comes to mind first.

_____
_____
_____
_____
_____
_____
_____
_____
_____
_____
_____
_____
_____
_____

THANK YOU

I would like to thank you for taking the time to read and learn from the lessons of love, liberty and pursuit of happiness expressed in this book.

I would like to thank self-help leaders Gabby Bernstein and Mastin Kipp for inspiring me to step onto this path as a leader, inspirer and teacher in my own unique, perfect way. Without you, I would never have seen another way to think, feel and believe in myself and my life. Thank you.

Thank you to my family - Mom, Dad, George, Jes - for never doubting my desires to make the world a better place. Because you told me I could, I did. And Dad, as you once told me, *"If you are happy, you are successful."* I will never forget that.

Thank you to God for inspiring this fire in my belly to be a light and help the world remember that it is love.

Thank you to my digital family for empowering this book to become a best-seller in its category and show people the power they already are and always have access to. That list is infinite. If you are reading this right now, rest assured, you are a member of my digital family and I thank you!

Thank you to the law of attraction for showing me that we are all more powerful, beautiful and special than we think.

ABOUT THE AUTHOR

Samantha "Sammy D" Davis is a motivational speaker and women's empowerment coach on the power of positive thinking with the goal to empower all women to feel beautiful, powerful, and special.

Throughout her career, Sammy has been a student of positive thinking, vedic meditation, and *A Course in Miracles,* a self-study curriculum for spiritual transformation. She is a student at the New York chapter of Philosophy Works and has completed transformational coursework with the Los Angeles chapter of Mastery in Transformational Training.

Sammy is leader of *SPARK SISTERS, a women's sisterhood circle which regularly meets in New York City for activities which fuel positive energy and attract positive creation.

In 2013 Sammy founded Lipstick Affirmations, a viral social media campaign of daily affirmations which share motivational message of self-love, and are each "sealed with a kiss" using her favorite shade of lipstick. She is also the founder of THE AFFIRMATION TOTE, an inspirational bag designed with the empowering affirmation, "I've let go of the need to be perfect today."

LOVE YOUR LIFE! is Sammy's second best-selling book, following *The 100 Best Vintage Shops Online 2013*. Sammy has been featured on national media including Arise TV, The Nate Berkus Show and *USA Today*.

Sammy currently spends time between New York City and Los Angeles and when not writing or lecturing, can be found meditating, running/swimming or secondhand shopping colorful and creative vintage fashion.

* * *

Find Sammy at SammyD.TV
Subscribe to her newsletter: tinyurl.com/sammydtv-newsletter

Instagram: @sammydtv
Twitter: @sammydavistv
Facebook: /iamsamanthamariedavis

* * *

Made in the USA
Middletown, DE
27 June 2015